AF600077

THE JUDICIAL SUMMONS

A Historical Synopsis and a Commentary

THE CATHOLIC UNIVERSITY OF AMERICA
CANON LAW STUDIES
No. 362

THE JUDICIAL SUMMONS

A Historical Synopsis and a Commentary

A DISSERTATION

SUBMITTED TO THE FACULTY OF THE SCHOOL OF CANON LAW OF THE CATHOLIC UNIVERSITY OF AMERICA IN PARTIAL FULFILLMENT OF THE REQUIREMENTS FOR THE DEGREE OF DOCTOR OF CANON LAW

BY

REV. VICTOR M. GOERTZ, J.C.L.
PRIEST OF THE DIOCESE OF AUSTIN

THE CATHOLIC UNIVERSITY OF AMERICA PRESS
WASHINGTON, D. C.
1957

NIHIL OBSTAT:

THOMAS O. MARTIN, Ph.D., S.T.D., J.C.D., LL.B., LL.M.

Censor Deputatus

Washingtonii, D. C., maii, 1955.

IMPRIMATUR:

LUDOVICUS J. REICHER, D.D., LL.D.

Episcopus Austiniensis

Austiniensii, maii, 1955

PRINTED BY: VON BOECKMANN-JONES CO., AUSTIN, TEXAS, U. S. A.

A

CRISTO REY

Dueño De Mi Vida

FOREWORD

The Code of Canon Law in its present form devotes an entire book[1] to the regulation of procedural practice for the authoritative settlement of matters in litigation, whether between physical or whether between moral persons. This facet of the social government—the exercise of judicial power—is governed in the canons which can be grouped under these general divisions: a) the notion of a trial and of ecclesiastical competence; b) the personnel of the courts; c) the rules governing the conduct of a trial; d) the parties to a trial with their various actions and exceptions; e) the progressive stages of a trial until the ultimate settlement; and finally f) the regulations for special procedures. That, at a glance, is the fourth book of the Code in its present form.

Many of the rules therein found are not of recent origin; in fact, it can readily be seen from the footnotes of the Code that the substance of these laws—whatever may have been their previous legal force—antedates by centuries, in some instances, the promulgation of the Code in 1918. For the most part the present legislation consists of such former enactments as were contained in the Papal Decretals, in the Acts and Constitutions of the Roman Pontiffs, in the Decree of the Councils and of the Roman Congregations, in the civil norms adopted by canonical laws and practice, etc.; however, these former enactments now receive their binding force directly and exclusively from the Code.[2] Thus the former discipline is no longer the immediate source of legal authority, but becomes a source of interpretation.[3]

Such is the principle enunciated in canon 6, namely that those

---

[1] Canons 1552-2194 inclusive—*Codex Iuris Canonici, Pii X Pontificis Maximi iussu digestus, Benedicti Papae XV Auctoritate promulgatus* (Romae: Typis Polyglottis Vaticanis, 1917) . . . (Hereafter simply the canon itself is cited).

[2] Cicognani, *Canon Law* (2. ed., Reprint, Westminster, Maryland: the Newman Press, 1949), p. 502 (hereafter cited as *Cicognani*).

[3] Cicognani, p. 499.

canons which restate the old law without change must be interpreted upon the authority of the old law, and therefore according to the interpretations already given by approved authors.

It is this rule of interpretation that receives frequent application in the study of the judicial summons or citation,[4] the initial stage in the development of the trial. Inasmuch as the rules of the Code governing this practice today are for the most part similar to, if not identical with, the old law, an understanding of the old is, in many cases, a sufficient commentary on the new.

Accordingly, in the treatise that is to follow, the consideration of the historical development in the practice of the judicial summons in ecclesiastical trials will not be separated from the commentary on the present law, but will be incorporated into it. The canons will be grouped under the headings of successive chapters arranged according to a logical and chronological development.

Prior to this detailed treatment on the law of citation, however, the various steps in the procedure of a trial will be briefly reviewed, according to the statement of the law, without extended commentary. After this, in the main body of this study, attention will be focused upon the summons, that initial step in the procedure of a trial.

The writer welcomes this occasion to express his sincere gratitude to His Excellency, the Most Reverend Louis J. Reicher, D.D., LL.D., first Bishop of Austin, for the opportunity of postgraduate study in Canon Law and for his generous assistance. The writer also wishes to thank the members of the Faculty of the School of Canon Law for their helpful assistance and scholarly guidance in the preparation of this dissertation.

---

[4]Attention is here called to the fact that the terms *summons* and *citation* will be used interchangeably throughout this work.

TABLE OF CONTENTS

Foreword vii

Introductory Notions xi

CHAPTER I

Necessity of the Summons 1

Article I. Historical Development 1

Section 1. *Roman Law Influence* 1

Section 2. *Ecclesiastical Development* 2

Article II. Present Rules 10

Section 1. *In Formal Procedure* 10

Section 2. *In the Exceptional Procedure of Canon 1990* 13

CHAPTER II

Form and Content of the Summons 19

Article I. Preliminary Notions and Definitions 19

Article II. Items to be Expressed in the Summons 21

Article III. The Peremptory Effect of the Summons 30

CHAPTER III

Service of the Summons 35

Article I. The Competent Judge 36

Article II. The Citation and the Bill of Complaint 39

Article III. The Parties to be Cited 40

Section 1. *The Individual Defendant* 40

Table of Contents—Continued

Section 2. *Minors, Incapacitated and Moral Persons as Defendants* 41

Section 3. *Number of Persons to be Cited* 47

Section 4. *Notice to the Plaintiff* 48

Article IV. Methods of Service 48

Section 1. *The Court Messenger* 49

Section 2. *Service Through the Mails* 56

Section 3. *Edictal Citation* 58

Section 4. *Canon 1724* 61

CHAPTER IV

EFFECTS OF THE SUMMONS 64

CONCLUSIONS 76

BIBLIOGRAPHY 77

ALPHABETICAL INDEX 81

BIOGRAPHICAL NOTE 82

INTRODUCTORY NOTIONS

Sketch of Successive Steps in the Procedure of Ecclesiastical Trials[5]

The first canon of the fourth book of the Code defines an ecclesiastical trial as the legal discussion and settlement before an ecclesiastical tribunal of a controverted matter on which the Church has the right to judge.[6] This will usually occur when some person, whether physical or moral,[7] seeking the vindication or the prosecution of a right or a declaration of some juridic fact prays the court to hear his case.[8] In such instances the trial is termed *contentious* and includes many types of cases as, for example, an irremovable pastor who, when illegally transferred, seeks the vindication of his injured legal rights, or again, a layman who, when unlawfully barred from the reception of the sacraments, asks for prosecution of his rights, or thirdly, an individual who, when forced into marriage, now petitions a declaration of nullity on the basis of facts constituting legal proof.

In addition to the foregoing contentious cases, there are criminal cases for the hearing of which the law likewise makes provision. These will usually find illustration in such instances wherein the laws of the fifth book of the Code are applied judicially either for the initial imposition of a penalty, or for the declaration of fact regarding the existence of a penalty already incurred at the time the law was violated. Thus for example, there could arise a case in which a pastor, having little regard for the wishes of the bishop, arouses the people with his sermons and conversa-

---

[5]This is not intended to be an exhaustive listing of the steps in a trial, but only a general view of the whole. Therefore no mention is made of such acts as the various mandatory decrees of the judge exercising jurisdiction.

[6]Nomine iudicii ecclesiastici intelligitur controversiae in re de qua Ecclesia ius habet cognoscendi, coram tribunali ecclesiastico, legitima disceptatio et definitio.—Canon 1552, § 1.

[7]Canons 87 and 99.

[8]Canon 1552, § 2, N. 1.

tions to join him in opposing the episcopal authority when he feels his rights have been violated. On the supposition that there are no bases in fact for the pastor's acts, one can envision a case in which the *Promotor Iustitiae,*[9] in the interest of the public good, could institute proceedings with a view to the judicial infliction of penalties.[10]

Whatever be the case—most often today in the diocesan tribunals in this country it will concern marriage—which is to be decided according to formal procedure, it will be reviewed within the framework of a trial composed of four major periods: 1) the introduction of the cause and the constitution of the process; 2) the construction of the process; 3) the definitive settlement; and 4) the execution of the sentence.[11]

In the first period of the trial, namely the introduction of the cause and the constitution of the process, these acts occur: The presentation of the plaintiff's petition and its acceptance by the court, followed by the citation of the defendant and the joinder of issue, wherein the matter in controversy is clearly specified. To illustrate these steps a hypothetical case can be presented.

A woman presents herself at the chancery, relates her story of marriage and divorce with allegations that the said marriage is invalid. She is ready to prove through witnesses and documents, that her husband did not intend a permanent union with her, and therefore she asks that a trial be instituted. If her case appears to have merit, she is assisted in stating her claims in a *libellus* (petition) drawn up according to the requirements of the law.[12] This petition is presented to the collegiate tribunal,[13] which according to law accepts it, and the order is given that the defendant, the husband, be cited. Accordingly, he is served with the summons[14] and the plaintiff is notified regarding the time when she is to appear.[15] On the appointed day the defendant,

[9]Canon 1934.

[10]Canon 2337.

[11]Beste, *Introductio in Codicem* (3. ed., Collegeville, Minn.: St. John's Abbey Press, 1946), pp. 809-810 (hereafter cited as *Beste).*

[12]Canon 1708.

[13]The number of judges varies for different causes—Canon 1576.

[14]Canons 1711-1725.

[15]Canon 1712, § 3.

who has been cited and informed in general of the nature of the cause, appears and denies the allegations of the plaintiff. The matter in controversy is determined, the issue is joined,[16] and the burden of proof rests with the plaintiff.[17]

The construction of the process, the second period of the trial, begins. During this stage of the trial the parties are interrogated, witnesses presented by the parties are examined, documentary proofs are studied. In general it is the period allotted for proving the allegations made in the petition or the bill of complaint presented to the court, and this is governed by the rather detailed rules given under the Title *De Probationibus*.[18] Illustration here would serve little purpose.

The definitive settlement of the cause, the third stage of the trial, embraces the following acts: the publication of the process, the conclusion of the cause, the final pleading and the sentence.

In the illustrative case presented the aforementioned acts would occur in this manner. By decree of the judge the parties or their advocates are informed, perhaps by letter, of their right to see the acts of the cause, e.g., testimonies of witnesses, and documents. If no further proofs are to be offered, or if the time allotted has run out, another decree of the judge closes the cause. After the closing of the cause, the judge gives the parties a proper interval of time, to be fixed at his discretion, to present to the court their defense or arguments either personally or through an advocate. Following that, the judges are called in for a discussion of the facts delineated in the course of the trial and a decision is rendered; after which, if appeal is to be made, it is done according to law.

In the event no appeal[19] follows the sentence, the fourth stage of the process is reached, that is, the execution of the sentence.

[16]Canons 1726-1731.

[17]Canon 1748.

[18]Canons 1747-1835.

[19]In nullity of marriage causes an appeal will always be made by the *defensor vinculi* when the sentence of the court of first instance stands against the validity of the marriage in question—Canon 1986.

CHAPTER I

Necessity of the Summons

Article I. Historical Development

Libello vel orali petitione admissa, locus est vocationi in ius seu citationi alterius partis.[1]

Once a bill of complaint or an oral petition has been admitted, the other party must be summoned to appear in court. While the obvious meaning of that text is that the service of the summons on the other party should follow the court's acceptance of the plaintiff's bill of complaint, further examination reveals that the juridical notion of this canon is not to be confined within the limits of that apparent meaning. The canon expresses more than is immediately obvious. Although it may seem no more than an expression of the rule that the other party be summoned at the time indicated, canon 1711 § 1, points to the fundamental necessity of having both parties present in the trial. If it be asked why one should read into the canon an idea of necessity which is not apparent at the first sight, the answer is that historically the summons was called for because of the recognized necessity that both parties be given a fair hearing. Since the canonical law on the summons is the heritage of centuries of judicial procedure, the roots of its interpretation strike deeply into past jurisprudence. Therefore examination should be made of these past sources with a view to what influence they have had on canonical development.

Section 1. *Roman Law Influence*

Roman Law, in addition to giving specific rules to govern the service of the summons, stressed the importance of citing the parties to trial. It recognized the natural right of defense, and it looked upon a trial as null if in it the opportunity to exercise

[1]Canon 1711, § 1.

this defense was lacking.[2] This idea of the necessity of the summons, for all practical purposes, was embodied in the very notion of the summons. Instead of being a quality externally imposed upon the notion of the summons, necessity came to be legally recognized as an essential property thereof.

Since that was the meaning of Roman Law, at least as applied in medieval canonical interpretation,[3] it has a bearing upon a correct understanding of the law as found today in the Code of Canon Law. The reason for this lies in the fact that there is a relationship between Roman Law and Canon Law on the procedure of judicial summons, a relationship that cannot be gainsaid, since it is so obviously preserved in the canonical use of the very words of Roman Law, *vocatio in ius*.[4] Since the retention of this ancient expression would have little purpose were it to be completely disassociated from its former meaning, it is only logical to understand the term *vocatio in ius* as expressive of a necessity formerly understood to be inherent in its meaning.

Section 2. *Ecclesiastical Development*

The medieval law and practice of the judicial summons, since it is substantially retained in the Code today, must be taken into consideration in a commentary on the present law. The necessity of the summons was expressed by Schmalzgrueber in words that

---

[2]"In the settlement of any affair it is fitting that judgment be rendered when all are present whom the case concerns; otherwise only those present are to be bound by the decision. If anyone, however, neglects his defense, after he has been cited, he is to be bound by the judgment rendered."—D. (42.1) 47; "An absent person should not be punished nor condemned; for the condemnation of anyone without having heard his case causes equity to suffer."—D. (48.17) (1.1); "To condemn someone who has not been peremptorily cited or to condemn him when the citation served did not reach him is to act invalidly."—D. (49.8) 1. C. Theod. (2.18) 1. (Translations made by the writer.)

[3]"The Church, owing particularly to the authority she enjoyed with rulers and nations had to elaborate a system of law, and seeing that certain provisions of Roman Law were well suited to her interests, these she adopted and canonized. This was especially evident with respect to the Roman Law regulations relating to judiciary action . . ."—Cicognani, p. 48.

[4]*In ius vocare est iuris experiendi causa vocare*—D. (2.4) 4.

bear similarity to the statement of the Code on this necessity.[5] He said that once the judge has accepted the bill of complaint, if the cause therein alleged seemed to be just, he was to proceed to summon the defendant. Moreover he held this summons to be so necessary, with reference to the absent party, that inherently *(per se)* every other judicial act would be null if the citation were omitted. Similarly Reiffenstuel[6] stated that the citation is so necessary with reference to the absent party that its omission renders the trial null. In the same place he further explained that the citation pertains to the natural right of defense, and should be denied no one; for no one is to be condemned without a hearing.

All these statements are certainly in keeping with the nature of a trial. By the very fact of litigation it is clear that each of the opposing litigants has an apparent right, at least, to the matter in controversy, and it is likewise evident that either one of the two litigants alone can present no more than his own claims and the reasons for them. If judgment were rendered on that basis alone, it might be argued that actually there has been no judicial decision, since it has not arisen from an authoritative comparison of the opposing claims. In other words, the court cannot be fully informed, if it has heard only one side of the question; neither can it be said that the defendant has been treated fairly, if he has not been given the opportunity to defend himself. From the very fact of litigation, doubt arises as to the rights of the opposing parties, and a solution rendered on the basis of the claims of the one without a consideration of those of the other is simply favoring the one, while it is clearly not settling the litigation. It is easy to see that the aggrieved party would have reason to raise exception to that decision. Recognizing this basic truth, positive law has long declared null and void

---

[5]Schmalzgrueber (1663-1735), *Ius Ecclesiasticum Universum* (5 vols. in 12, Romae: ex Typographia Rev. Cam. Apostolicae, 1843-1845), Lib. II tit. 3, n. 15 (hereafter cited Schmalzgrueber).

[6]Rieffenstuel (1624-1703), *Ius Canonicum Universum.* (7 vols., Parisiis, 1864-1870), Lib. II, tit. 2, n. 67 (hereafter cited as Reiffenstuel).

a judicial process which does not take into consideration[7] both sides of a question.

An example of just such a provision of positive law is found in the *Decretum* of Gratian.[8] It reads in part: *Caveant iudices ecclesiae, ne absente eo, cuius causa ventilatur, sententiam proferant: quia irrita erit. . . .*[9] The judges of the Church were warned that they should not pass sentence in the absence of a party to the cause, since such a sentence would have no validity. Stronger emphasis could hardly have been placed upon the necessity of the parties' appearance in the trial than the threat of complete nullity for a sentence pronounced despite their non-appearance. That the presence of the parties to a trial was the prime concern becomes clear from a simple reading of the canon. To evaluate properly, however, its full import, one must view it in its historical setting as it was then understood. The most complete contextual setting in which to view this canon with intent to grasp its historical meaning is a spurious letter attributed to Pope Eleutherius.[10] The letter itself was made up largely

[7]This consideration is given as long as all the legal opportunities to present his case are afforded to the defendant, regardless of his neglect or refusal to avail himself of them.

[8]C. 2, C. III, q. 9.

[9]A clue to the actual origin of this text is the fact that Pseudo-Isidore placed its beginning with a fourth Council of Carthage, as did Ivo before him. For that reason it may have come from a collection which, according to the common opinion, was made in France about the middle of the fifth century. The reference was to the *Statuta Ecclesiae Antiqua,* which collection was falsely ascribed to a fourth Council of Carthage (a. 398), and was said to be composed of material from the councils of the Greek Church, the councils of France and the decrees of Roman Pontiffs.—Cf. Hinschius, *Decretales Pseudo-Isidorianae et Capitula Angilramni* (Lipsiae, 1863), p. 304 (hereafter cited as Hinchius); S. Ivo, *Decretum,* VI, c. 319 in *Opera Omnia* (Excudebatur et veniat apud J. P. Migne editorem, 1855), Tom. I, p. 510—Migne, *Patrologiae Cursus Completus, Series Latina* (221 vols., Parisiis, 1844-1864) (hereafter cited *MPL*). Concerning the so-called fourth Council of Carthage cf. Van Hove, *Commentarium Lovaniense in Codicem Iuris Canonici,* 1 vol. in 5 toms., Tom. I, *Prolegomena* (2 ed., Mechliniae-Romae: H. Dessain, 1945), pp. 152-153 (hereafter cited *Prolegomena*).

[10]Hinschius, p. 126; Mansi, *Sacrorum Conciliorum Nova et Amplissima Collectio,* (53 vols. in 60, Parisiis, 1901-1927) Vol. I, p. 695 (hereafter cited *Mansi*).

of a Roman Law text[11] and therefore an appreciation of its interpretation will contribute to understanding the historical meaning of this so-called letter, and give a broader view of the canon under consideration. In the interpretation attached to the Roman Law cited, it was said that the judge, once he had begun a case, was patiently to hear the allegations and replies of the parties litigant, always allowing a complete discussion. In keeping with this rule he was not too quickly to pass sentence; in fact, he was frequently to ask questions, so that the case might be better known. The reason was: *si apud ipsum finienda causa est, totum debet agnoscere.* Such then were the reasons, as understood by the medieval writers, for the presence of the parties in the trial. The judge was to be fully informed on the cause before passing sentence, and for that reason the parties were to be present.

This emphasis on the necessity of the parties' being present for the trial was an indirect argument for the necessity of the summons, for historically that was the method of effecting the defendant's appearance. As one medieval author expressed it: "one who has not been warned or cited is not to be judged."[12]

Since the sentence was null when the defendant was not cited, it followed that he could not be compelled to abide by the void decision. There could follow no execution of the sentence. Ultimately, then, the execution of the sentence with reference to the defendant took its force from the juridical fact that he was initially subjected to the court by the summons, and thus given an opportunity to present his claim, for comparison with the plaintiff's allegations, on the basis of which, the court was to come to its enforceable decision.

In practice the summons did not always have any immediate connection with the execution of the sentence. In fact, under

---

[11]C. Theod. (2.18) 1.

[12]Arnulphus (a canonist of Paris between the years 1250-1254), *Die Summa Minorum,* II Band, II Heft, p. I ff.—Wahrmund, *Quellen Zur Geschichte des romisch-kanonischen Processes im Mittelalter* (4 vols. Innsbruck: Verlag der Wagner'schen K.K. Universitäts-Buchhandlung, 1905-1928) (hereafter this collection is cited as Wahrmund, and the individual work is cited by its full title).

the old law, as well as under the present legislation, there were causes in which an execution of the sentence was not required.[13] Whenever it was needed, however, the necessity of the summons in the form of a preceptive notice depended upon the type of the cause. If the court had initially summoned the defendant and given him the opportunities of defense, with the result that a valid decision was rendered, it did not have to require his presence in the execution of the sentence, which entailed the disposal of a material *res,* or the determination of the status of persons. Provided the defendant's rights had been duly safeguarded, his presence was not required for the execution of a valid sentence to dispose of the heretofore controverted property now in the possession of the court. In the determination of the status of a person the execution of the sentence, for the most part, would be inherent in the publication of the sentence.[14] In both cases the defendant has had the opportunities of defense by reason of the summons, and has had notification of the decision of the court in the publication of the sentence. If he does not make use of the remedies available to attack the sentence, he is bound by the decision rendered in his cause by the court to which he was subjected by the summons; and the execution of that sentence, for which his presence is not necessary, can be carried out without further notice to him.

Under the present law, whatever notice is required for informing the defendant of his obligation to comply with the sentence is to be governed by the rule of canon 1724. If after this it becomes necessary to punish the defendant for contempt of court, the usual rules on contumacy are to be followed.

Thus it was that medieval canonists and later authors emphasized the necessity of the summons by pointing with repeated insistence to the nullity which resulted in practice from an omis-

---

[13]Cf. Wernz-Vidal, *Ius Canonicum ad Codicis Normam Exactum,* (7 vols. in 8, Romae: Apud Aedes Universitatis Gregorianae, 1923-1938), Vol. VI n. 657, footnote n. 2 (hereafter cited Wernz-Vidal). Coronata, *Institutiones Iuris Canonici* (editio altera aucta et emendata, 5 vols., Taurini-Romae: Marietti, 1939-1947), Vol. III, p. 360 (hereafter cited Coronata).

[14]This is said with the understanding that no personal action is required of the defendant by reason of a decision against him.

sion of the summons, a nullity which was understood by some to embrace the entire trial.[15]

Equal emphasis of a similar kind is not lacking in the Code of Canon Law.[16] If nullity results from the fact that the citation is not properly drawn up or legitimately served, it will surely result from the fact that the citation is omitted altogether. Noone,[17] in his commentary on canon 1723 together with canon 1894, n. 1, states that "the summons is so necessary that, if omitted, or if it lacks the elements required by law, or if it is not lawfully served, the subsequent acts of the process and the ensuing sentence are remediably null." Substantially the same is the commentary of Wernz-Vidal,[18] stating that the citation is so necessary that the entire process together with the sentence, when pronounced against an absent party, is *ipso iure* null and void when the citation has been omitted.

There are exceptions in which the citation will not be required simply because the need for it has ceased. Canon 1711, § 2, states: If the contending parties appear before the judge of their own accord to plead their cause, it is not necessary to issue the summons . . .[19] Two principal ideas are expressed in the text. These must be verified in fact before one can dispense with the summons in virtue of this canon. First of all the party must appear of his own accord, and therefore if anything other than his own initiative caused an individual to appear, there would be barred all application of the rule stated in canon 1711, § 2. For instance, a man learns through gossip of a trial in which he is the defendant, and, under the false impression that he must appear in court—although he is not yet cited—presents himself at the trial. The judge, feeling that he has of his own accord appeared

[15]Schmalzgrueber, *loc cit.;* Reiffenstuel, *loc. cit.*

[16]*Si scheda citatoria non referat quae in canone 1715 praescribuntur aut non fuerit legitime intimata, nullius momenti sunt tum citatio tum acta processus.*—Can. 1723.

[17]*Nullity in Judicial Acts,* the Catholic University of America Canon Law Studies, n. 297 (Washington, D. C.: The Catholic University of America Press, 1950), p. 81.

[18]Wernz-Vidal, *De Iudiciis,* Vol. VI, n. 383.

[19]*Quod si partes litigantes sponte coram iudice se sistant ad causam agendam, opus non est citationi . . .*

to argue his cause, omits the citation. If later on the defendant can prove that he was not willingly in court, he may lodge an exception to the validity of the process because of the lack of the citation.[20]

A variation of the example just presented could occur if a defendant under a like false impression appeared in court, but learned almost immediately of the possibility of raising an exception. Wishing, however, to upset the cause if a decision unfavorable to himself is rendered, he waits until after the sentence and then raises an exception to the validity of the process by reason of the lack of the citation. Such an individual, although initially present not of his own accord, seems to remain of his own accord, because the reason for his continuing presence now arises from his own intention; however, the reason for his stay—namely the desire ultimately to frustrate the results of the trial by raising an exception to its validity—is such as to render dubious his right to lodge such an exception, if it be supposed that his presence is not of his own accord. This is so by reason of canon 1628, which states that dilatory exceptions, especially those which have reference to personages and the manner of the trial, must be proposed and ruled on before the joinder of issue, unless they shall have emerged only afterwards, or the party raising the exceptions affirms under oath that he did not until then have knowledge of them. In the cause in question knowledge of the possibility of an exception[21] arose after the joinder of issue, which was the time when it should have been presented, for it seems the intent of the law that an exception be made at the time it arises.[22] It is true that the law[23] speaks of the right of raising an exception as being by nature perpetual; however, this per-

[20]Wernz-Vidal explain the nullifying effect of the illegally composed or executed citation, and their explanation applies to the lack of the citation as well: "Si reus ad citationem nullam compareat, quasi ea teneretur ob ignoratum citationis nullitatem, videretur dicendum omnes actus processuales posteriores infici nullitatis vitio, cum canones 1711 & 1723 exigant *validam* citationem vel *spontaneam* comparitionem, qualis non est ea comparitio, qua per errorem putatur obligatoria.—Ius Canonicum, Vol. VI, n. 393, nota 48.

[21]*Exceptio processualis*—Beste, p. 796.

[22]Canon 1628.

[23]Canon 1667.

petuity of right to raise an exception is not itself an indication that any given exception is well founded. The fact is that the burden of proof rests with the one lodging the exception. In the cause in question it is unlikely that the defendant could show any convincing argument in his favor inasmuch as he did not avail himself of his right within the legally defined limits regarding dilatory exceptions. The judge in ruling against him will not be overthrowing canon 1667, which speaks of the perpetual right to raise an exception, but will be ruling against the delay in raising the exception, which the judge can do in virtue of canon 1628.

A second condition which must be verified in warrant of the application of canon 1711, § 2, is that the party's appearance must be for the purpose of pleading his cause, and not simply coincidental to the fact of a progressing trial in which he is involved. Thus, for example, a man appearing at the chancery or tribunal for the sole purpose of a social call is obviously not presenting himself to plead his cause in a trial, which incidentally is being instituted against him.

This understanding of the canon according to its obvious meaning is in keeping with the teaching of the pre-Code authors,[24] who stated that one who is already present need not be cited, unless he needs time to prepare his cause. In such instances, when the party is already present, the summons would serve to indicate the time and place for appearing.[25]

Gratian and the authors before the Code gave other reasons which rendered unnecessary the service of the summons. The most commonly accepted of these reasons obtained in any cause in which the perpetrated crime was so known to all that it did

---

[24]Reiffenstuel, op. cit. Lib. II, tit. 2, n. 69. Schmalzgrueber, Lib. II, tit. 3. n. 15; Pirhing, (1606-1679), *Ius Canonicum in Quinque Libros Decretalium* (5 vols. in 4, Dilingae, 1722), Lib. II, tit. 2, n. 227 (hereafter cited as Pirhing).

[25]Lega, *Praelectiones in Textum Iuris Canonici, De Iudiciis Ecclesiasticis* (4 vols., Romae: Typis Vaticani, 1896-1901), Lib. I, Vol. 1, p. 430 (hereafter cited as Lega).

not admit of any defense.[26] The principle underlying their opinions was expressed by Lega (1860-1935) in these words: *Ius enim naturale non exquirit rei defensionem, cum possible non est,* and it is easily understood; however, its application to practice was fraught with difficulty. No doubt it was for this very reason that Pirhing as well as Reiffenstuel[27] suggested that the judge would do well to cite the defendant even in causes of notorious crimes, especially if there be the possibility of any defense. This precautionary measure, Pirhing stated, would obviate the possibility of nullity in the process and the definitive sentence, if in fact the summons should have been served. Thus in its application this opinion of the authors regarding the omission of the summons in certain criminal causes was very limited. It is not incorporated in the Code, and is not applicable today.

In addition there are other reasons[28] which rendered the summons unnecessary but, unlike that of the party's spontaneous appearance, are not mentioned in the Code, and for that reason seem not to have equal applicability to present day practice.

Article II. Present Rules

Section 1. *In Formal Procedure*

For the most part the summons is a constitutive element of formal procedure in the conduct of a trial, and it is in that setting that an application of the law concerning its necessity is first made.

---

[26]*Manifesta accusatione non indigent*—c. 15, C. II, q. 1; Pirhing, Lib. II, tit. 2, n. 227; Schmalzgrueber, Lib. II, tit. 3, n. 15; Reifenstuel, Lib. II, tit. 2, n. 72; Lega, Lib. I, Vol. I, p. 430.

[27]*Loc. cit.*

[28]1) If the defendant maliciously hides; 2) if the defendant is suspected of flight or there is danger in delay; 3) if the defendant has little possibility of defense; 4) if one be only incidentally connected with the cause; 5) if in criminal causes sentence is passed in favor of the absent party; and 6) in all causes in which the cause proceeds without the solemnities of a judicial trial, a sentence *lata pro reo absente non citato* is valid, so that in all those causes the summons was to be considered as unnecessary.—Pirhing, Lib. II, tit. 2, n. 227.

In the usual nullity of marriage[29] cause it will be necessary to cite[30] the defendant as well as the defender of the bond for the joinder of issue. Failure to do so in either case will result in nullity of the process. This is clear from the fact that the article of the Instruction is intended to be an application[31] of canon 1711, § 1, to the particular circumstances of marriage causes, as well as from the explicit ruling of canon 1587 with regard to the defender of the bond; on the other hand, as the spontaneous appearance of the defendant will obviate the nullity resulting from the lack of citation[32] so also will the presence of the defender of the bond, despite his non-citation, have the same saving effect.[33]

In regard to that particular type of marriage cause in which the *Promotor Iustitiae ex officio*[34] initiates proceedings, there is a particular ruling on the necessity of the summons which states that both consorts are to be cited.[35]

In the light of all that has been said thus far regarding the necessity of the summons as well as the clear statement of the Instruction *Provida,* it is difficult to envision that the conduct of a formal trial in a nullity of marriage cause would allow the omission of the summons in instances other than that already mentioned, namely the exception of canon 1711, § 2.

If the location of the defendant is unknown, for instance, the

---

[29]To cite a few examples: Causes dealing with impotence, with the factors force and fear, with an intention *contra bonum prolis,* etc.

[30]Instructio *Provida,* ex aedibus Sacrae Cong. de Disciplina Sacramentorum, die 15 Augusti anno 1936, Article 74 (hereafter cited by the article) .–Text found in Coronata, *Institutiones Iuris Canonici,* Vol. III, p. 655; Canon 1711 § 1.

[31]The purpose of the Instruction is stated in its introductory decree: *In hisce regulis iudices ipsi et tribunalium administri praecipuos canones de processibus agentes accurate apteque dispositos reperient, necnon brevem facilemque eorundem explanationem, ex iurisprudentia praesertim erutam atque ex Normis S. R. Rotae, quo plenius ipsis iidem Codicis canones, quibus derogatum non est, sint perspecti, eosque expeditius singulis aptare possint matrimonialibus causis.*

[32]Canon 1711, § 2.

[33]Canon 1587.

[34]Canon 1971, § 2, n. 2.

[35]Article 75 of the Instruction *Provida.*

necessity of the summons does not cease, as is evident from the fact that the Code provides a method of citation in such instances.[36]

Even when it would be impossible for the defendant to appear in court, e.g., he is in prison for life, the summons is not to be dispensed with. As has been said, a party is to be given a hearing, an opportunity to defend himself, and his appearance personally in court is not absolutely necessary for the exercise of that right. It is true that some discussions of this matter have placed emphasis upon the idea of the presence of the parties in the court. It is clear, however, that the fact simply of their appearance is not the ultimate desired. The presence of the parties, particularly of the defendant, is sought *in order that* they may prosecute or defend their rights; therefore the impossibility of appearing is really the loss of a means of defense, and it does not connote the cessation of the right itself. All this is contemplated in the law, and a practical solution of the cause in which the defendant is detained in prison could be found within the provisions of the law on procurators and advocates.[37] The judge would cite the defendant and require that he appoint a procurator, possibly from a list supplied by the court, to appear in his behalf. Failure to make this appointment, although this is not explicitly treated in the law, could render the defendant contumacious according to the canons.[38]

In many instances today the defendant will live far from the court which has the competence to hear the cause; nonetheless the necessity of the summons is not thereby removed. The right of the party to defend himself is not affected by so accidental a feature as distance . . . it remains with the individual wherever he may be.

Historically[39] the liability of a defendant to be summoned to a court other than the one of his own territory was accepted,

---

[36]Canon 1720, § 1.

[37]Canons 1655-1666; Article 74, § 4, of Instruction *Provida.*

[38]Canons 1842-1851; canon 1646 uses the word *respondere,* but this does not necessarily mean that it must be done personally. Moreover the right of the plaintiff to have his case heard is not to be denied because of the impossibility on the part of the defendant personally to appear.

[39]C. 2, *de sententia et re iudicata,* II, 11, *in Clem.*

although discussion[40] did not evidence unanimity of opinion regarding the manner in which this was to be done. The present Code by the very fact that it makes provisions for citing a person who lives separated from the court by great distance[41] indicates *de facto* the necessity that such a person be cited.

Section 2. *In The Exceptional Procedure of Canon 1990*

Canon 1990 states in part: *Cum ex certo et authentico documento quod nulli contradictioni vel exceptioni obnoxium sit, constiterit de existentia impedimenti disparitatis cultus . . . simulque pari certitudine apparuerit dispensationem super his impedimentis datam non esse, hisce in casibus, praetermissis sollemnitatibus hucusque recensitis, poterit Ordinarius, citatis partibus, matrimonii nullitatem declarare, cum interventu tamen defensoris vinculi.*

In reference to the question of the citation, only its necessity in this summary process and the consequences of its omission are here to be considered. Discussion is to center principally on the question whether a failure or a neglect to cite the parties will invalidate the process, will render it null and void.

A simple reading of the text of the canon leads to no decisive conclusion. The words *citatis partibus* certainly indicate that the parties are to be cited, but they do not, in themselves, show that invalidity will result when the summons is omitted. The text may be further considered by way of an examination of its application in the Instruction of 1936.[42] Article 227, § 1, has the words *citatis semper partibus iisque auditis* instead of the words *citatis partibus* as found in the canon. At first reading one is struck by the greater emphasis placed upon the summoning of the parties. Moreover, there is an indication of the reason for the summons—that the parties be heard. This stated reason is certainly consonant with the historical thought on the necessity

---

40*Glossa* ad c. 2, *de sententia et re iudicata,* II, 11, in Clem; Lega, Lib. I, Vol. I, p. 434; Bouix, *Tractatus de Judiciis Ecclesiasticis* (2 vols. Parisiis: apud Jacobum Lecoffre et Socias, Bibliopolas, 1855), Tom. II, pars. 2, p. 161 (hereafter cited Bouix).

41Canon 1719.

42Instructio *Provida.*

of the parties' presence in the trial and on the threat of invalidity if the parties were not given a hearing.[43] The emphasis of the Instruction, however, as well as its statement of the purpose of the summons does not clearly call for invalidity when the summons is not served, although perhaps there is a hint at this. To constitute a nullifying law, however, more is required.[44] The text of canon 1990 by itself, therefore, more by default than by express statement, argues to the validity of the summary process, even when the summons has not been served; on the other hand, the text cannot be said positively to exclude invalidity. It remains a possibility, and a possibility that has some basis in law as is now to be examined.

One must turn to the context in the hope of a clearer understanding of the law. Canon 1990 is found in the Fourth Book of the Code, which deals with procedures. The first part *(Pars Prima)* of this Book deals with trials *(de iudiciis);* the second part *(Pars Secunda),* with the process of beautification and canonization; and the third part *(Pars Tertia),* with the handling of particular cases and the application of penal sanctions. Canon 1990, the summary process, is found in the first part *(Pars Prima),* the part which deals with judicial procedures.

The pertinent question now turns upon the significance of this position in the context of rules for judicial procedures. The most obvious interpretation is that this summary process has some relationship to the ordinary judicial procedure, the judicial trial. That is true, and the relationship fundamentally is that the process of canon 1990 is likewise a judicial process.[45] Basically then it is to have all those essential elements which make up the formal trial. In short, by reason of the context, it is to be governed by the rules of the context wherein it is found, unless other provisions be made.

Canon 1990 tells what these other provisions are. First, with reference to the rules of evidence there is a departure in the

---

[43]*Supra,* p. 4: c. 2, C. III, q. 9.

[44]Cf. Canon 11.

[45]Reply of the Pontificial Commission for the Authentic Interpretation of the Code, 6 Dec., 1943—Acta Apostolicae Sedis, Commentarium Officiale (Romae, 1909-) XXVI, 94 (hereafter cited as *AAS).*

summary process from the rules of an ordinary trial. Second, with reference to the practice in the trial the canon makes it permissible to omit certain solemnities which must be employed in the ordinary trial. With reference to the citation, however, the canon states explicitly that the parties must be cited. This it does after it has said that there are solemnities which may be omitted, namely certain solemnities as they are found in formal trials. The fact that the citation is mentioned in this way could be understood as dissociating it from the phrase which allows the omission of solemnities; however, that is not the only interpretation. The specific mention of the citation after the exempting phrase, *praetermissis sollemnitatibus hucusque recensitis,* may be understood in two ways at least.

First, the word *sollemnitatibus* could as well be interpreted to embrace whatever solemnities are connected with the formal summons, while the words *citatis partibus* indicate that the summons is substantially to be retained. Second, in the other interpretation, the specific mention of the summons as well as its place in the canon (1990) may be looked upon as dissociating the citation from the possibility of being omitted in virtue of the phrase *praetermissis sollemnitatibus . . .*, that is, that it is not a solemnity which may be omitted even in this summary process.

According to the first interpretation it is necessary only that the summons substantially be had, and whatever solemnities are usually involved in its formation or service may be omitted. This is the opinion of Doheny,[46] who says, "it can safely be stated that all the detailed formalities enunciated in canon law need not be observed in the summoning of the parties. However, some form of notification which is truly adequate is necessary. Hence the provisions of canon 1715 must be duly observed." That is his interpretation, and a reasonable one; for in view of the fact that the law is considering a summary process, and in view of the fact that it allows solemnities not essential to a judicial process to be omitted, the opinion which would allow the omis-

[46]*Op. cit.*, Vol. II, p. 125.

sion of formalities in the service of the summons would surely seem to fit into the general context of the law.

The substantial element in the citation, as regards its formation, is clearly and adequately stated in canon 1715. The essential or substantial element of the service of the summons is some sort of notification to the party concerning that which is stated in the citation. Since canon 1990 allows the omission only of solemnities, it is understood that the substantial elements must be preserved in the practice of the summary process. For the same reason it is to be understood that the lack of the summons, as in the formal trial, will render null and void the ensuing process.

In the second interpretation, the specific mention of the citation is taken to mean that it is dissociated from those acts which may be omitted in virtue of the canon. Since in this interpretation it is mentioned without any regulatory modification, the citation is understood to be governed by the ordinary rules given in the earlier canons for the judicial service of the summons. Were this not the meaning of the law, then it seems that other specifications would have to be made. The presumption, by reason of context, is that the usual rules apply. Under this interpretation it is clear what is to be done. The formulation of the summons and its service will follow those rules and, since they provide for invalidity when the summons is not served, the summary process likewise will be null when the summons is lacking.

Another line of argument which leads to the conclusion that the summons is necessary for the validity of the process, although not an argument for the necessity of following the usual rules, may be constructed in this manner: Those elements which constitute a trial or a judicial process are necessary for the validity of a summary process;[47] but the summons is one of the constitutive elements of a judicial process, and therefore the summons is necessary for the validity of the summary process.

Historically it seems that the summons was considered in this

---

[47]Cf. Bouscaren, Canon Law Digest, (3 Vols., Milwaukee: The Bruce Publishing Company, 1942-1954), Vol. III, p. 603.

light, namely as being necessary to the substance of the judicial process. In the authoritative statement,[48] wherein Clement's stated purpose was to clarify the rules in this summary procedure, it was said that the *necessity* of such acts as the formal bill of complaint, the joinder of issue, etc., ceased. On the other hand, it was specified that the cause was not to be so abbreviated as to allow the omission of *necessary* proofs and defense, and the citation was, by no means, to be dissociated from those causes which were to be heard in summary fashion. In explaining the *necessity* just referred to the commentators[49] spoke of it as referring to those acts which are necessary to the substance of the trial. In the context, then the citation clothed with this notion of necessity was understood as belonging to the substance of the trial.

In examining the present law one can argue indirectly to the conclusion that the summons pertains to the substance of the judicial process, the trial. In the canon law the trial is referred to as a dispute, a *disceptatio,*[50] which by its nature implies opposites. In ecclesiastical trials this opposition exists between physical or moral persons,[51] the plaintiff and the defendant. These are necessary elements in such a trial. The plaintiff by the act of presenting his bill of complaint to a competent court submits himself to that court. The defendant, on the other hand, is subjected to the hearing and the decision of that court only by the legitimate summons (or also by an appearance made on his own initiative). Until the defendant is so subjected to the court, there will be no trial, no *disceptatio;* and he will not be bound by the court's decision, *definitio.*[52] For that reason, therefore, the summons is spoken of as pertaining to the substance of a trial, as being a substantial element. If it be lacking, there is no trial.

One may conclude from the discussion just ended as well as from the preceding one that 1) in general the summons, basically

[48]C. 2, *de verbi significatione,* V. 11, in Clem.

[49]*Glossa Ordinaria* ad c. 2, *de verbi significatione,* V, II, in Clem, s. v. *necessario.*

[50]Canon 1552, § 1.

[51]Canon 1552, § 2, n. 1.

[52]Cf. canon 1552; also canon 17, § 3.

considered, is necessary to the substance of a trial, and that the nullity of the summary process, which arises when the summons is lacking, is radically founded in the reason that the summons is a constitutive element of a trial, a judicial process; 2) the rules to be followed in the formulation and the service of the summons for this summary process are only those whose fulfillment is necessary to the substantial formulation and service of the summons. Finally, the sanction of invalidity, as enacted by the positive law, applies equally to the summary process, when the summons is lacking.[53]

[53]Cf. "first" interpretation presented above. Doheny states: "If the citation happened to be invalid, the sentence would be invalid only in virtue of remediable nullity, which could be rectified without considerable difficulty."—*Op. cit.* Vol. II, p. 125. The same might be applied to the situation when the citation is lacking altogether.

CHAPTER II

Form and Content of the Summons

Article I. Preliminary Notions and Definitions

Roman Law of the time of Justinian defined citation as the call to appear for the purpose of legally testing a right.[1] Without going into any technical exposition of the foregoing definition, one can see its similarity to the one given by a post-Tridentine author,[2] who defined the summons as a judicial act whereby the judge's legitimate command is served upon the party required to be present for the hearing of the cause. This is an accurate definition which embraces the legal source of the citation, the command of the judge, as well as its function, namely the mandatory notification, together with its purpose, that is, the party's appearance in the trial.

The division of the summons made by the pre-Code authors[3] has been adopted, for the most part, by authors after the promulgation of the Code.[4]

Noval (1861-1938), perhaps, indicated as complete a division as any in the following manner: The summons is divided *ratione auctoris: a iure, ab homine; ratione subiecti: generalis,* whereby all interested parties are summoned to trial, and *specialis,* whereby a specific person is cited; *ratione formae: personalis directa,* served upon the party by a public minister of the court, and *personalis indirecta,* served upon the party through an

---

[1]*In ius vocare est iuris experiendi causa vocare*—D. (2.4) 4.

[2]Pirhing, Lib. II, tit. 2, n. 212.

[3]Pirhing, Lib. II, tit. 2, n.n. 213-215; Santi, *Praelectiones Iuris Canonici,* (4 ed., 5 Vols., Ratisbonae, 1903-1905) Lib. II, tit. 3, n. 4; Bouix, *Op. Cit.,* Vol. II, p. 549; Lega, Lib. I, Vol. I, p. 432.

[4]Lega-Bartoccetti, *Commentarius in Iudicia Ecclesiastica iuxta Codicem Iuris Canonici* (3 vols., Romae: Anonima Libraria Cattolica Italiana, 1950), Vol. II, p. 526; Noval, *Commentarium Codicis Iuris Canonici,* Lib. IV, *De Processibus* (2 vols., Romae: Augustae Taurinorum, 1920-1932), Vol. I, p. 284; Wernz-Vidal, Vol. VI, n. 380.

intermediary, such as a member of the family; *ratione effectus: simplex,* which does not render its violator contumacious until it has been served a third time, and *peremptoria,* which renders its violator contumacious even when it has been served but once; *ratione executionis: verbalis et edictalis.* Although a division such as this is not expressly given in the Code, its various elements enter into present canonical application, as will be seen especially in a subsequent chapter devoted to a study of the service of the summons.

Now, however, attention is centered upon the nature of the summons, as currently understood. Certainly there has not been any notable change from the earlier teaching regarding either the general descriptive notion of the summons or the more elementary understanding of it. Pirhing's[5] general description of the citation, namely that it is the beginning and the very foundation of the whole judicial process, remains accurate today even as does his more precise definition already cited. Perhaps as accurate as any definition is that of Wernz-Vidal, stating that the citation is a judicial act whereby the defendant, at the instance of the plaintiff and under the authority of the judge, is called to trial for the purpose of litigation.[6]

Basically, then, the summons is a command emanating from a jurisdictional authority that is being exercised in a judicial process. Unlike the private nature of earlier forms of citation,[7] the summons today in Canon Law exists only in the realm of

[5]*Loc. Cit.*

[6]Citatio est actus iudicialis, per quem reus, actore rogante, iudicis auctoritate, litis peragendae causae in iudicium vocatur.—Vol. VI, n. 380.

[7]Citation in its early Roman Law *(XII Tables)* provisions was a private matter. "The process in a real action began with a summons by the plaintiff to the defendant, the prescribed form of which (if any) we do not know, to appear in court—*in ius vocatio.* As it was essential to the *legis actio,* as a mode of litigation, that both parties be present and play their part, obedience to the summons could be compelled." There were probably excuses from obeying. "If the defendant evaded *in ius vocatio* by trickery or flight, the creditor might seize him, which probably means bring him by force to the magistrate's court."

Buckland, *A Text-Book of Roman Law* (2 ed., Cambridge: at the University Press: 1932), p. 610.

public acts. It is not the private individual who summons the defendant to court; rather, it is by the authority of the court itself that the defendant is so cited. It is immediately obvious that not all matters of litigation will be of such a nature as to concern the public good, and that a controversy can arise over matters of cnly private interest; nonetheless, even in the latter event a party to the cause does not serve the summons on the other, but leaves it to the court whose authority has been invoked to hear the cause.[8]

Article II. Items to be Expressed in the Summons

A consideration of the summons embraces an analysis of its ultimate constitutive elements as well as an examination of its functional purposes. Looking to the origin of the summons, one sees that it rests in the public authority here and now specifically being asserted in the command of the judge. All the consequences envisioned in the proper working of the summons find the initial reason of their existence in the command of the judge, so much so that without that command no other phase in the detailed plan of citation will be executed. If the judge gives not the order, the citation will not be drawn up; if he gives no order, the court messenger will not deliver the citation. Thus the citation, in its present canonical form and functional application cannot be thought of as existing unless it has been initiated by an order of the judge. This is clear from canons 1715 and 1723, which demand for validity that the command of the judge be expressed in the written form of the citation.

The question may be raised: must the command of the judge, which for validity is to be included in the written form of the citation,[9] be stated perceptively, or may it be expressed in the form of an invitation. In other words, may the citation in some instances read: "You are asked to appear" instead of "you are ordered to appear"? The text of the canon[10] reads that the com-

---

8Canon 1706.

9Canons 1715 and 1723.

10. . . quae praeceptum iudicis parti conventae factum ad comparendum exprimat . . . Can. 1715, § 1.

mand of the judge is to be made known to the party required to appear, and not that an invitation to appear is to be made known to the party by reason of the order of the judge. It seems therefore that the formal citation is to be not only informative, but preceptive; that, in addition to giving notice to appear, it is to indicate the obligation to comply. To fulfill the requirement of the law therefore the citation must always in some way be expressive of a command.

Not many commentators discuss this particular question, and the few who do so hardly do more than offer a single comment. Wernz-Vidal[11] state that the order of the judge does not cease to be such when for reasons of urbanity it is couched in the words of an invitation. It is clear that they, too, understand that the law requires that the citation shall not lose its preceptive nature, although they allow it to be stated in a mild form. Likewise Roberti[12] states that this order of the judge commanding a party to appear may be expressed in the form of an invitation, so long as its preceptive nature is not lost. The practice suggested by these opinions can be followed provided it is truly a precept that the citation expresses, and not *merely* an invitation. Whatever form, therefore, can be said to cite the party, and not merely invite him, is in keeping with the law. Such was the mind of the compilers of the Code. In their discussion preliminary to the final codification this problem was reviewed and a text prepared, which was to make it allowable to invite a party to the trial instead of citing him[13] if circumstances so warranted. This para-

---

[11]*Ius canonicum*, VI, n. 386, footnote n. 36.

[12]*De Processibus* (2 vols., Romae: Apud Aedes Facultatis Iuridicae ad S. Appolinaris, 1926), Vol. I, p. 437.

[13]Here follow the schema of the development of text and the note on its final rejection:

Schema D: *In facultate iudicis est in aliquibus casibus, pro sua prudentia, formali citationi invitationem ad comparendum substituere, servatis tamen regulis pro citationis denuntiatione statutis.*—Caput II, canon 195, § 3.

Schema E: *In facultate iudicis est in aliquibus casibus, sive attenta qualitate personarum sive natura causae, pro sua prudentia formali citationi substituere invitationem ad comparendum.*—Caput II, canon 205, § 3.

Schema F: Si *quando personarum qualitas vel causae indoles id suadeat,*

graph was finally deleted, and for that reason one must now hold that all who are to be called to trial must be preceptively cited, and not merely informatively invited, although the citation may be stated in the form of an invitation as long as the precept is not completely hidden.

One can envision a cause in which the defendant is quite embittered against the Church and certainly does not recognize its judicial authority. It may be that the judge or the judges are highly desirous that this man appear in court, but fear that the service of the summons will only turn him away. What is to be done? Certainly the summons is to be served upon him; the necessity of this has been seen. Also the precept of the judge must be expressed, at least in some manner that does not exclude it. Therefore the judge might have the citation worded in this way to express his order: "You are asked to appear in court." This can be understood to be a polite way of saying "you are ordered to appear," and therefore would fulfill the requirement of the law, while perhaps being less provocative of antagonism.

After a statement of the order of the judge canon 1715 next requires that the name of the judge be mentioned. The least that this can mean is that the Tribunal be named. The reasons for the present law are similar to those of the old,[14] namely that the citing judge was to be made known through the citation, so that the party summoned might ascertain whether he was competent or not. If a judge lacks competence, the party summoned, under the present law,[15] has the right to raise an exception. In such a

licebit iudici invitare partes potius quam eas citare.—Caput II, canon 178, § 3.

Footnote about the rejection of these formulae: *Censet non expedire pro qualitate personarum citandarum distinguere inter citationem et invitationem. Si utraque vox easdem iuris consequentias parit, non est cur fiat distinctio. Iudex non debet esse personarum acceptor: iam vero esset, si alios citaret, alios invitaret ad iudicium. Nemo obstringitur invitationi morem gerere. Citatio autem est actus iuridicus, cui citatus obsequi obligatur, nisi velit contumaciae sequelas experiri. Suadeat igitur ut § 3 deleatur.*—*Codicis Iuris Canonici Schemata* (Lib. IV, *De Processibus*, digessit Franciscus Roberti, Typis Polyglottis Vaticanis, in civitae Vaticana, 1940), pp. 204-205.

[14]Pirhing, Lib. II, tit. 2, p. 95; Santi, Lib. II, tit. 3, n. 7.

[15]Canons 1610 and 1611. In the matter of lodging an exception against the

case the defendant must appear; for it is not his right to ignore the summons by reason of his opinion that the judge is incompetent. To ignore a valid summons[16] on that basis alone is equivalently to render a decision on the judge's competency. It is clear that the litigant has no such right in law to pass judgment on the judge's competency. The defendant must respond to the valid summons in some way. The Instruction Provida in article 89, § 1, seems to rule out complete passivity on the part of the defendant; he must, at least, make known his exception to the judge's competency. Through lodging his exception the defendant is giving at least negative recognition to the authoritative force of the valid summons and to the obligation on his part to respond.

By the very fact that this right can be exercised against each member of a collegiate tribunal as well as against an individual judge, it seems properly indicated that the names of all the judges who take part in the hearing of the cause be mentioned in the citation. The old law, as evidenced by the authors[17] required that the judge state in the citation whether he acted with ordinary or with delegated power. In the latter event it was necessary that a copy of the delegation be attached to the citation; otherwise the party was not obliged to obey. This was based upon the juridical reason given by Innocent III (1198-1215) [18] namely that no one was obliged to respond unless he was shown evidence of the Apostolic mandate by which supposedly he was commanded. Similarly in the Code delegated judges must clearly

---

judge the provisions of the Code bear some similarity to the Roman Law, which stated that the judge himself was to determine whether he had jurisdiction and whether the party summoned was to appear. Thereupon the party could lodge his exception, if he thought the judge incompetent.—D. (5.1) 5.

[16]The summons is valid when it is drawn up according to the rule of canon 1723. Competency does not figure in as one of the essentials required for a valid summons. The question of competency can be legally raised after the valid summons has been answered.

[17]Pirhing, Lib. II, tit. 2, n. 216; Reiffenstuel, Lib. II, tit. 2, n. 56; Schmalzgrueber, Lib. II. tit. 3, n. 3; Bouix, Vol. II, p. 549; Lega, Lib. I, Vol. 1, p. 433.

[18]*Glossa ad* c. 31 X, *de officio et potestate iudicis delegati.*, I, 29, *casus.*

demonstrate the fact and the authenticity of their delegation. Canon 1606 states that delegated judges are obliged to observe the rules stated in Canons 199-207 and in 209. Canon 200, § 2 is particularly applicable here. It has the rule that the burden of proof rests on him who makes the assertion that he is empowered to act by reason of delegated power.

Without going into a lengthy discussion on competence one can summarily state that anyone who is incompetent, whether absolutely or relatively, can issue a valid summons, but such an act is open to exception, which can be lodged against his jurisdiction. Reiffenstuel[19] stated in this regard: *Reus coram incompetente iudice conventus impune non comparet.* He added, however, that the defendant's exception to the competence of the judge must be lodged before the joinder of issue. If this defendant, knowing of the incompetence, does not raise an exception and the cause proceeds, he is understood to have accepted the judge and consented to the cause's progression.

Next the law requires that the nature of the litigated cause be made known, at least in general terms, in the citation. The obvious reason for this is that the defendant may become informed regarding the cause that is being pleaded against him. An old rule stating this fundamental reason was incorporated in the Decretal legislation:[20] *"In citatione . . . talia sint expressa per quae plene (reus) possit instrui super quibus indicio convenitur."* This corresponds to the statements that the citation must assure each one's having an opportunity to protect his rights, and must specifically afford the defendant an opportunity to decide upon a course of defense.[21] Regarding this statement of the nature of the cause in the citation, Pihring[22] noted that it was a recommended practice, though not required, that the bill of complaint be included with the citation. Santi (1830-1835)[23] attested to the fact that this practice was followed, and added

---

[19]Lib. II, tit. 2, n. 7.

[20]C. 2, *ut lite pendente nihil innovetur,* II, 5, in Clem.

[21]C. 4, C. V, q. 2.

[22]Lib. II, tit. 2, n. 219.

[23]Lib. II, tit. 3, n. 4.

that certainly it met the requirement of the law that a statement of the nature of the cause be included with the citation.

Today in the law of the Code,[24] alternate methods for drawing up the citation are proposed, and both include sending the bill of complaint with the summons. Coronata[25] remarks that the Code seems to insinuate that this is a better and safer way, but he adds that the observance of this rule is not required for validity. This is surely the correct doctrine, for canon 1712 does not contain an invalidating clause similar to that of canon 1723. This does not mean that the law may be ignored; it simply means that there can arise reasons which will excuse from its observance. For instance, a nullity of marriage cause is presented. Through personal knowledge the judge is cognizant of the rancor existing between the parties. Further, he is aware of the fact that the defendant has pledged to upset the cause. In order therefore to withhold from this defendant the fuller knowledge that could guide him in preparing his fictitious defense, the judge will dispense with sending the bill of complaint, and in the citation submit only a general statement regarding the cause. This is not without foundation in authoritative sources. In stating the norms for hearing and deciding criminal as well as disciplinary causes of clerics in America the Sacred Congregation for the Propagation of the Faith ruled that a detailed account of the alleged accusation was to be included in the citation to the defendant. If, however, the nature of the cause suggested greater caution in the statement regarding it, then only a general description needed to be given.[26]

Next in the written summons the names and surnames of the parties, namely the plaintiff and the defendant, are to be given. If for no other reason, this would be necessary in order that it be clearly established in the record of the court who are involved in this litigation and who shall be bound by the authoritative decision. In causes of a private nature the name of the

---

[24]Canon 1712, § 1.

[25]*Institutiones*, Vol. III, p. 149.

[26]S. Cong. de Prop. Fide, a. 1883—*Collectanea S. Congregationis de Propagande Fide* (2 vols., Romae: Typographia Polyglotta, 1907), Vol. II, p. 169, n. 1586 (hereafter cited as *Collectanea*).

plaintiff is required, in order that the defendant may know that he is being cited at the instance of another party, and not by the judge alone.[27] According to Reiffenstuel and Schmalzgrueber a judge acted invalidly if in a cause of a private nature he summoned the defendant on his own initiative, and not at the instance of the plaintiff. This, too, seems to be the sense of canon 1618.

The obvious reason for the defendant's[28] being named in the citation is that he become properly identified and unmistakably notified of his obligation to appear. An additional reason given by Schamlzgrueber[29] is that it is impossible to institute proceedings for contumacy or for the execution of the sentence when there is no determination of the party against whom to proceed.

The requirement of the Code that the place in which one is to appear must be stated in the summons is traditional and follows the traditional interpretation. The nullity which attaches

---

[27]Schmalzgrueber, Lib. II, tit. 3, n. 4; Reiffenstuel, Lib. II, tit. 2, n. 58; Pirhing, Lib. II, tit. 2, n. 218; Bouix, Tom. II, p. 161; Canon 1618.

[28]Who can be cited as defendant? Cf. Canons 1646-1654. "All baptized persons are subjects of the Church of Christ, and are therefore amenable to its authority. With the exception of the Roman Pontiff such persons are directly subject to the judicial power of the Church. Baptized non-Catholics are in principle not exempt from ecclesiastical jurisdiction. Doubtfully baptized persons are presumed to be subjects of the Church when the doubt concerns the validity of the administration of baptism, for the validity must be presumed until the contrary is proved. If the doubt concerns the fact of administration, then recourse to circumstantial presumption is in place, but if all bases for these are lacking, then such persons are not to be considered as subjects of the Church. Non-baptized persons are not directly subject to the Church, and therefore cannot be summoned to appear as defendants in ecclesiastical trials."—Krol, *The Defendant in Contentious Trials,* The Catholic University of America Canon Law Studies, n. 146 (Washington, D. C.: The Catholic University of America Press, 1942), p. 7. *"Hinc infideles omnes penitus exempti sunt a potestate ecclesiastici magistratus, videlicet tanquam rei conveniri nequeunt, qualibet de causa, coram tribunalibus Ecclesiae."*—Ottaviani, *Institutiones Iuris Publici Ecclesiastici* (3 ed., 2 vols., Civitate Vaticana: Typis Polyglottis Vaticanis, 1947-1948), Vol. I, p. 288, n. 160. Indirectly the unbaptized may be subject to the ecclesiastical judicial power by reason of connection with matter over which the Church has control.—Decree of the S.C.S. Off., January 27, 1928—AAS, XX (1928), 75.

[29]*Ius Ecclesiasticum Universum,* Lib. II, tit. 3, n. 5.

to a summons deficient in this regard had its initial legal force in canon law under Decretal legislation,[30] which likewise freed one from the obligation to appear in a place that was dangerous by reason of pestilence or war.[31] This Decretal law, which bore similarity to the Roman Law,[32] namely that one who had been ordered to appear *in aliquem locum inhonestum* could with impunity refuse to appear, continued in post-Tridentine practice. The question whether this is applicable in the Code today is open to discussion. The law is this: one who is legitimately cited is bound to appear.[33] When therefore a judge has a summons drawn up according to the requisites of the law and served upon the party in legal manner, that person is legitimately cited and is bound to respond. This does not mean, however, that he is obliged absolutely; reasons may arise which, for a time at least, may excuse from the obligation. Such a situation seems to obtain when one is summoned to an unsafe place. This reasoning is not without legal foundation, for the law is cognizant of the fact that a proportionate reason *(iusta causa)*[34] may arise which will excuse the party from appearing.

The old law also stated that the party was not obliged to appear, if he was summoned to a place outside the jurisdiction of the citing judge,[35] and with due allowance made for certain exceptions[36] this remains applicable in the Code today.[37] The judge must summon the party to a place within his jurisdiction. Ordinarily this will be the place designated by the bishop for the tribunal, which will usually be found in or near the chancery or at least in the episcopal city. It is not forbidden, however, that the party be summoned, in an individual case, to some other place within the limits of the judge's jurisdiction. This is true

[30]C. 43, X, *de rescriptis,* I, 3.

[31]C. 10, X, *de sententia et re iudicata, II,* 29.

[32]D. (4.8) (21.11).

[33]Canon 1646.

[34]Canon 1842.

[35]Pirhing, Lib. II, tit. 2, n. 220; Reiffenstuel, Lib. II, tit. 2, n. 62—*extra territorium ius dicenti impune non paretur.*

[36]Canon 1637.

[37]Canon 201, § 2.

by reason of the law whereby the judge can delegate a priest in the distant reaches of the diocese to act as judge. Implied in that authorization to delegate is the power to designate a place, other than the usual tribunal, to which someone may be summoned. If in the summons the place is not mentioned, the usual place of the tribunal is to be understood. Such is the teaching of the early authors.

Finally the summons must state clearly the time at which the party is to appear, that is the year, the month, the day, and the hour. According to Reiffenstuel[38] the time must be "certain, just and opportune." Certainly the lack of any statement regarding the time at which the party is to appear would be an integral defect in the summons and would render it invalid. A like invalidity could be urged for all omissions of mention of the hour, unless the Ordinary, according to canon 1638, had determined the regular hours for the court sessions. In that event any lack of specifying the hour will not cause invalidity, since the hour has already been legally fixed. This is based upon the same reasoning as that already given, namely that the place of the tribunal previously designated according to law is to be understood when no place is mentioned in the citation. If the court summoned a party to appear on a day when judicial procedure is prohibited, the party would be obliged to appear, but might raise an exception to the court's action. This could easily be overruled, however, if the court were so acting because of necessity, charity, or for the public good.[39]

The time within which the cited party must appear is not stated in the present canon law. It seems therefore that this determination is left to the discretion of the judge, who in following the old law principles,[40] even though the law itself has changed, will allow greater or lesser time in accord with the varying circumstances, such as the place of the trial, the distance to be traveled and the condition of the persons involved.

Finally, hardly more need be said than that the summons drawn up according to these rules is to be stamped with the seal

[38]Vol. II, Lib. II, tit. 3, p. 262.

[39]Canon 1639, § 1.

[40]D. (5.1) 72; *glossa ordinaria ad* c. 6, C. XXIV, q. 3, s.v. *Peremptorio*.

of the tribunal and signed by the judge or his auditor and the notary. If the cause is to be heard by a collegiate tribunal, the presiding judge is to sign the summons.[41]

Article III. The Peremptory Effect of the Summons

Once it is drawn up according to the requirements just indicated, the citation needs to be served only once on the party.[42] Failure to obey this order to appear in court can render the party summoned contumacious. Such is the sense of canon 1714 when it states that every citation is peremptory.

This differs from the old law, wherein the civil law was adopted[43] which itself allowed a choice of procedures in this matter. One method involved the service of three citations upon the party, and these cumulatively considered rendered the party contumacious if he culpably neglected to appear; the other method, which was more the exceptional procedure, consisted of one citation which was expressly peremptory.

The Code, however, calls for one citation, of a peremptory nature, which by itself can render the disobedient party con-

---

[41]Beste, p. 812.

[42]For an exceptional case see canon 1845.

[43]Interpretatio ad Paulum, 5.5A.7 (5.5.6 Brev.) Haenel, *Lex Romana Visigothorum* (Berlin, 1849), p. 240. This section in the *Sententiae* of Paulus reads: *Trinis litteris vel edictis aut uno pro omnibus dato aut trina denuntiatione conventus nisi ad iudicem, ad quem sibi denuntiatum est aut cuius litteris vel edicto conventus est venerit, quasi in contumacem dicta sententia auctoritatem rerum indicatarum obtinet: quin imo nec appellari ab ea potest.* On this law cf. Wenger, *Institutes of the Roman Law of Civil Procedure* (Revised ed., Veritas Press, New York, 1940), p. 281, footnote 38. Cf. C. (7.24) (1.9); c. 6, C. XXIV, q. 3.—In the latter text the principle is enunciated: "*quia nemo propere vel praepostere, scilicet non commonitus neque convictus est iudicandus.*" In the additional explanation little doubt can remain about the connection of Roman Law and Canon Law: "*De conventione autem huiusmodi imperatoris manifestorum criminum lex dicit: 'Quicumque tribus auctoritatibus iudicis conventus, vel tribus edictus fuerit ad iudicem provocatus, aut uno pro omnibus peremptorio, id est quod causam extinguit, fuerit vocatus, et praesentiam suam apud eum iudicem, a quo ei denunciatus est, exhibere noluerit, adversus eum quasi in contumacem iudicari potest. Quinimo retractari nec per appellationem negotia possunt, quotiens in contumacem fuerit indicatum.'*"

tumacious. This does not mean to say that the fact of non-appearance subsequent to legal service of the summons begets certainty with regard to the fact of contumacy. It is one thing to say that objectively contumacy exists, but another thing to prove that it exists in the individual in question. Therefore in a given case a party may be in contempt of court after the service of the summons, but another citation may be necessary to prove that contumacy.[44] The law does not state that this must be done; it merely suggests reiteration of the citation as a means of proving contumacy. In the event, however, that the judge wishes to force obedience to the court by the threat of penalties, he must issue a second summons with the threat of penalties.[45] These two exceptions, then, to the legal requirement of one citation, arise not from a failure of the one citation to render the disobedient party contumacious, but from the possibility or the need either to prove or to break contumacy already existing by reason of disobedience to the one citation.

Since the one citation required by law is of a peremptory nature, it may be asked whether a clause stating that it is so and warning that disobedience will constitute contempt of court needs to be included. The answer is not immediately obvious. Because of the fact that canon 1715 does not require the inclusion of a statement regarding the peremptory nature of the summons, there seem to be reasons for saying that it is not required. In addition to that, another argument can be raised in view of the fact that it is not necessary for each citation expressly to identify itself as peremptory. It is a legal presumption that subjects are not ignorant of the law which binds them;[46] therefore all are presumed to know that each citation is of a peremptory nature. Historically the same was understood of the Roman Law enactment[47] which was adopted in the Canon Law. Reference is made to the three citations issued at stated intervals. Although none was expressly a peremptory summons, the service of the three legally effected the peremptory result. On the other

[44]Canon 1843, § 2.

[45]Canon 1843, § 2.

[46]Canon 16, § 2.

[47]C. (7.24) (1.9).

hand, it must be remembered that the presumption stated in canon 16, § 2, is open to contrary proof by reason of the same canon. In actual cases it will probably be a rare individual who will know the law in this matter; it is more likely that the majority could prove ignorance and upset the presumption. In so doing they may be able to establish a just cause for absence, be free of contumacy, and have available for them the use of several remedies[48] against the action already taken. In order to forestall the delay which could thus be occasioned, it seems properly indicated to state explicitly in the summons that any culpable failure to comply with its order will render the disobedient party contumacious.

Intimately connected with the foregoing discussion is the question whether the summons must *actually* come to the knowledge of the party cited before it will have its effect. The Code makes no explicit statement on this point; however, it is obvious that the general purpose of the laws on citation includes its reaching the parties for whom it is intended. On the other hand, it is also clear that the law authorizes procedure in causes when there is no certainty that the summoned party has received the summons. More will be said on this point later.[49]

A glance at earlier discussions reveals that this same problem was reviewed, and that no unanimity of opinion existed. Ioannes Teutonicus[50] in concluding a treatment of these divergent opinions stated: "According to many the sentence is valid even though the peremptory citation did not come to the knowledge of the defendant. Hence it seems sufficient for the pro-

---

[48]1) *Remedium contra declarationem contumaciae ante sententiam: purgatio, quae fit quando pars in contradictorio demonstrat impedimentum adfuisse ne se sisteret in iudicio;* 2) *remedium post latam sententiam: restitutio in integrum ad appellandum. Hoc remedium praesto est ei qui purgavit contumaciam post sententiam definitivam* (can. 1847).—Goyeneche, *De Processibus* (1 Vol. in 2 parts, Romae: ad Ioannis Lat.), Vol. I, pt. 2, p. 119.

[49]Cf. Chapter on edictal citation, p. 58.

[50]He composed the *Glossa Ordinaria* to the *Decretum* between 1211 and 1215.

nouncement of the sentence that the defendant has been adequately cited, although he has not been found."[51]

That which John had held to be the representative opinion actually became law in the Decretals of Gregory IX.[52] There it was stated: "If a person's adversary has been legitimately cited but fails to appear, spurns to appear, or even absents himself, his procurator, if he left one, is to be cited. . . . If this is done, the witnesses for the other party can be heard and the sentence passed." Although it could be more specific, it is the second part of that canon which contains the view that the citations need not come to the knowledge of the party cited. The law merely presumed that the party would learn of the citation and acted upon the legal strength of that presumption without reference to its factual realization. This is borne out by a second text of the Decretals.[53] There is an instruction to an archbishop about clerics who did not observe the law of residence, it was stated: "If you do not know the whereabouts of a cleric, you are to cite him by means of three edicts published at his church. If he does not return within six months, he is to be deprived of his church." Again the law seemed to presume that the party cited would acquire knowledge of the summons. Furthermore, inasmuch as the hearing of the cause was to be continued even without reference to the factual realization of that presumption, the conclusion is that the summoned party's knowledge of the citation was not absolutely necessary.

While the old law did allow for the hearing of causes when the peremptory citation did not come to the knowledge of the cited party, it also sought to keep the rule flexible enough, so that it would not hinder an equitable judgment when the party had a reason for his continued absence. That certainly is what the glossator[54] had in mind when making this final remark: "This much is certain. Whether the citation has or has not reached the cited person as long as he is able by proof to adduce a righteous cause for his absence, all that has been done in the

[51] *Glossa Ordinaria,* ad c. 2, C. III, q. 9, s.v. *Caveant.*

[52] C. 3. X, *de dolo et contumacia,* II, 14.

[53] C. 11, X, *de clericis non residentibus,* III, 4.

[54] *Glossa Ordinaria,* ad c. 2, C. III, q. 9 s.v. *Caveant.*

cause will be retracted." This stemmed from a Roman Law rule given in the Title, *De in integro restitutione,*[55] wherein a response was given concerning the question of helping an individual who, while absent, had suffered loss: "Although nothing solemnly done is easily to be changed, nevertheless, when equity evidently demands such a change it should be made." Applied to the completed trial this rule provided that one who was absent through no fault of his own was to be restored to his former position in spite of the fact that he had been cited, but had not appeared.

Much the same rule is applicable in the Code today. In canon 1720, for instance, the Code provides for a summons when the defendant cannot be found. Since these are the circumstances of the edictal citation, it is very unlikely that the judge will know with certainty that the summons has come to the knowledge of the party. Unless one is to render the rules on the edictal citation meaningless, however, this is not to say that the cause may not proceed; for the edictal citation is to be understood as having, in its own peculiar circumstances, the same effect as other methods of citation in initiating the process. In this event, therefore, as in others, the judge may proceed to declare contumacy and proceed with the hearing of the cause. Of course this is said with the understanding that the party who proves that his absence arose through righteous cause is freed of contumacy.

---

[55] D. (4.1) 7.

CHAPTER III

Service of the Summons

Thus far the law has been concerned more with the structural elements of the summons; now attention turns to the functional purposes of the legally formulated citation and their intended realization. As has been seen, and can be seen in the content of the summons, it is intended to bring the party cited, principally the defendant, to trial. Both the necessity and the purpose of the summons, inherently expressed in its content, are to have their effectual realization in the service of the summons. Thus the rules on this procedure are really rooted in that fundamental necessity which calls for the summons as a practical means of insuring a proper protection of rights. The law recognizes that fact and accordingly attaches to the violation of the procedural rules which govern the service of the summons a sanction of invalidity. This invalidity infects all the subsequent acts of the process and also the final sentence itself[1] when the law is violated. As will be seen, however, compliance with the law is not to be identified with the fulfillment of its purpose, for it can happen that all the requirements of the canons are met, but the party cited will not appear in court. The rules on service of the summons are intended to bring about that effect, but their observance is not completely bound up in its realization.

Basically the service of the summons is rather simple procedure. Its central act is the delivery of a legitimate citation to the party being summoned. Whatever methods are devised by the law for the regulation of this action, they add nothing to its essential notion. Thus the variations that one finds in the procedural rules on the service of the summons arise from the diversity of situations to which the law adapts this practice.

Pre-Code authors[2] spoke of the service of the summons as in-

---

[1]Canons 1723 and 1892.

[2]Verano, *Juris Canonici Universi Commentarius* (5 vols., Monachi, Sumptibus ac Typis Joannis Jaechlini, Typographi Electoralis et Biblipolae), Vol.

volving these elements: the order of the judge, the execution of that order by the court messenger in the delivery of the citation, and the notation in the acts of the proceedings that the party has been duly cited. Though all these elements are necessary for the effective working of the summons, principal among them is the order of the judge. Without his authorization the subsequent acts of the delivery of the summons as also the notation in the acts will have no validity. Although it has not always been thus, it is nevertheless an old law[3] that one was not obliged to appear except when commanded by the judge. Since the summons contains a precept of the judge which proceeds from jurisdictional power, one can immediately see that an unauthorized person has no power to serve the summons with any juridical effects. He must be commissioned to do so by the judge.

Article I. The Competent Judge

No change from the old law has taken place in the Code. In fact, in the process of codification the old law has been reiterated and further clarified. The express statements in the preliminary drafts of canon 1712 regarding the authority of the judge[4] were not included in the text of the Code, but the present text *citatio fit a iudice* is to be understood as indicating that the authority of the judge initiates the service of the summons.[5] Certainly it does not mean that the judge himself performs the physical act of serving the summons, for the law makes other provisions for that. If the phrase, *fit a iudice,* is to mean anything, then it must be that the summons comes into being and is served upon the individual by reason of an authoritative decree of the judge.

II, p. 284; Pihring, Lib. II, tit. 2, n. 222; Lega, Vol. I, Lib. I, part 1, n. 407, p. 433.

[3]*Neminem iudicio exhibendum esse praecipimus, nisi de cuius exhibitione iudex pronuntiaverit.*

[4]*Sola iudicis aut tribunalis praesidis auctoritate citatio ad iudicium subeundum iuberi potest.*—Schema A, can. 199, Roberti, *Schemata,* p. 206.

[5]This must be so inasmuch as the citation is an act of jurisdiction: C. 11, X, *de probationibus,* II, 19; *Citatio est actus iurisdictionis contentiosae et coactivae.*—De Angelis, *Praelectiones Juris Canonici* (5 vols., ad methodum Decretalium Gregorii IX Exactae, Romae et Parisiis, 1877-1891) Tom ult., pars 1, p. 153.

It is clear that in those instances when only one judge hears the cause it is he alone who orders the service of the summons; on the other hand, questions may arise with reference to those instances when a collegiate tribunal hears a cause. Does the presiding judge or the entire tribunal order the citation of the parties, particularly the defendant, for the joinder of issue? A fundamental principle is stated in regard to those instances in which a cause is heard by a collegiate tribunal,[6] namely that it is to proceed in a joint manner; this, however, seems to have reference to the passing of the sentence. At least in a negative way canon 1892, n. 1, indicates that this joint action of the collegiate tribunal is required for validity only in the pronouncing of the sentence. Reason exists therefore for saying that the decree ordering the citation and its service need not originate immediately in the collegiate action of the tribunal, at least as regards its validity.[7] This much can be said, that implicitly the tribunal assents to or authorizes service of the summons in its acceptance of the bill of complaint, for once that has been done the other party must be cited.[8] Substantially then the authority of the whole tribunal will always underlie the summons issued in a cause being heard in a collegiate manner, even though it be only the presiding judge who signs the written decree ordering that it be done. It can be added that this action on the part of the presiding judge does not go beyond the general rule that he is to "direct the process and determine what is necessary for the administration of justice in a cause."[9] In this interpretation the phrase "direct the process" is to be understood even of its inception through the service of the summons for the joinder of issue.

Against this, however, and in support of the opinion that the word *iudice* of the canon does not mean the presiding judge, of the collegiate tribunal as well as the individual judge in cases

[6]Canon 1577, § 1.

[7]Roberti states with reference to the Presiding Judge that he is empowered *iubere citationes partium.—De Processibus,* Vol. I, n. 105, p. 175.

[8]In marriage causes—*a pari* in other causes requiring collegiate action—it is by the joint action of the tribunal that the bill of complaint is accepted.—Article 61 of the Instruction *Provida.*

[9]Canon 1577.

heard by one, is the fact that the name of the presiding judge was mentioned explicitly in the preliminary drafts[10] of the Code, but omitted in the final wording. By the very fact that separate provisions to indicate the presiding judge's authority to cite the defendant were proposed one can see that the Commission working on the codification took cognizance of the question here being discussed. What significance is to be attached to the ultimate elimination of that provision? Is it to mean that the term *iudex* includes the presiding judge, or is it to mean that the presiding judge is excluded from authoritatively initiating the service of the summons?

The answer, perhaps, is suggested in other considerations. When speaking of the judge, the law in a given cause has in mind either an individual or a collegiate body. The latter, of course, is constituted of individual members, no one of whom, individually considered, however, is the judge in those causes which require joint action. It is the corporate body acting as such that performs those judicial acts which depend upon the authority of the judge. Since, therefore, no contrary provision is anywhere made, it is by the authority of the collegiate body, in the particular cause at trial, that the order for the service of the summons is given.

Somewhat as a supporting argument it may be urged that the judge, here the collegiate body, which must pronounce the sentence[11] should have authorized the initiation of the process. Now, the process begins with the service of the summons. Therefore the collegiate body should order the service of the summons. Moreover the collegiate tribunal by its joint action must accept the bill of complaint.[12] It seems *a fortiori,* that by its corporate authority it should begin the process. Therefore it appears to be the better opinion to hold that, in those causes which are to be heard by a collegiate tribunal, the decree ordering the service of the summons should originate in the corporate action of that body.

---

[10]*Si causa tribunali collegiali reservata sit, citatio fit ab ipso praeside tribunalis.*—Roberti, *Schemata, Schema* B, can. 82, 2, pp. 206 and 207.

[11]Canon 1892.

[12]Article 61.

It is easy to see that in practice a similar discussion would not have to arise. The judges are convened and the bill of complaint is presented to be considered with reference to acceptance or rejection. It meets all the requirements, the tribunal decides that it is competent, and that the person has the right to present his cause. All the judges agree that the bill of complaint be accepted and prepare to proceed with the cause. They decide that the defendant is to be cited and that the plaintiff is to be notified of the developments and told of the time when he is to appear. Memoranda of these acts are to be drawn up, signed and preserved in the acts of the cause. The citation is then issued over the signature of the presiding judge acting for the collegiate body.[13]

Article II. The Citation and the Bill of Complaint

Canon 1712 next speaks of the citation being written either on the page whereon appears the bill of complaint, or on a separate page to be affixed to the bill of complaint. Either method may be used; the choice of one or the other rests with the judge, for he is not obliged to choose one in preference to the other. This is evident from the very fact that the indicative mood is used. The law is suggesting a practical manner of serving the summons without imposing any obligation that it be done in one exclusive way. In many causes therefore one would have to do no more than write at the bottom of the bill of complaint the order of the judge citing the party, indicate the place and the time for appearing, affix the seal, and obtain the proper signatures for the legally formulated summons. In other causes, however, such as may call for edictal citations, it would be a matter of prudence, at least, to draw up a summons with only a general statement of the cause.

Much the same rule existed in the old law. Sending the bill of complaint with the summons was not required by the law, but was recommended as a worthwhile practice.[14] Some felt, however, that a very general statement regarding the cause would

[13]Article 76, § 2.

[14]Pirhing, Lib. II, tit. 2, n. 219; Reiffenstuel, Lib. II, tit. 3, n. 61.

suffice in criminal causes.[15] Thus it is left to the discretion of the judge to send the bill of complaint with the summons or to have only a general statement regarding the cause in the text of the summons. If this latter method is used and the bill of complaint is not sent with the summons, no invalidity will result.

Article III. The Parties to be Cited

Section 1. *The Individual Defendant*

The second paragraph of canon 1712 states that the summons is to be served upon the defendant and, if there be more than one, each is to receive a citation. Throughout this present study and in the context of these canons[16] attention is focused on the defendant who has in some way injured or hindered the rights of the plaintiff. He is therefore summoned and given an opportunity to defend himself against the charges of the plaintiff.

Usually in a given cause the defendant will be identified in the bill of complaint. The judge, therefore, in his initial consideration of competence must decide whether he is competent with reference to the defendant; for as Beste[17] says, the competent forum is that tribunal which is endowed with the requisite power to hear the cause both with respect to the matter proposed and with respect to the party whom the plaintiff would cite as defendant. The law creates exemptions in this regard, so that certain individuals cannot be cited as defendants in the courts from which they are legally exempt.[18] In those instances the inferior judge is absolutely incompetent,[19] and his summons could be ignored with impunity by the defendant. This does not mean to say that the incompetence of the judge affects the validity of the summons; but rather that the defendant, who has responded to the valid summons of an incompetent judge, has the right to raise an exception to that incompetence. If the defendant does not raise an exception to that judge, the judge will

[15] Schmalzgrueber, Lib. II, tit. 3, n. 6; Bouix, Tom. II, pars, 2, p. 161.

[16] 1711-1725.

[17] *Introductio in Codicem*, p. 778.

[18] Canons 1556 and 1557.

[19] Canon 1558.

proceed validly in hearing the case, although illicitly in those instances when he is only relatively incompetent.

Section 2. *Minors, Incapacitated and Moral Persons as Defendants*

The rules which have been stated with reference to the defendant as an individual apply with equal validity to the corporate body whose role is that of a defendant, as well as to certain types of defendants now to be considered.

Canon 1713, for instance, states that if the defendant is a person who does not have the free administration of the goods concerned in the controversy, the summons must be presented to that person who in his name must answer in the trial, according to the rules of canons 1648-1654. As Coronata[20] rightly notes, the defendant here referred to is determined in the provisions of canons 1648-1654. Thus it becomes necessary to study those laws in order to make sure that the summons will be served upon those only who have the legal capacity to act as a defendant.[21]

Canon 1648, § 1, states that parents, tutors and guardians are bound to plead or defend the causes of minors and persons without the use of reason. If the judge thinks that the rights of such persons are in conflict with the rights of the parents, tutors or guardians, or that they live at so great a distance from the parents, tutors or guardians that the latter cannot at all, or can only with great difficulty, represent their charges in court, a guardian *ad litem* is to be appointed by the judge. However, in spiritual causes or in causes connected with spiritual affairs, minors who have attained the use of reason can act either as plaintiffs or as defendants without the consent of the parent or tutor. If they

---

[20]*Institutiones,* p. 150, Vol. III, footnote n. 1.

[21]Introductory to his treatment of these canons Krol in his dissertation remarks: "Juridic capacity, in virtue of which a person can be a party to a trial, is not the same as procedural capacity, in virtue of which a party in a trial can personally posit procedural acts which produce their proper juridic effects. The latter presupposes and completes the former, but is not a necessary consequent of it." *The Defendant in Contentious Trials,* p. 66. Thus in the present consideration an individual may have rights, but, legally, in virtue of canon 1713, may not be cited personally to defend those rights.

are fourteen years of age, they can in person plead their cause, but otherwise they must plead through a tutor appointed by the ordinary, or by a tutor chosen by the minor with the approval of the ordinary.

In the application of canon 1713 therefore it is the parents, the tutors, the guardians, or the procurators who are to be summoned. The citation is not to be served upon the party who is actually the defendant, but upon his legally designated representative. In the citation this representative must be properly indicated by name and surname as well as by the title under which he is summoned.[22]

Since moral persons, both collegiate and non-collegiate, are regarded as on a par with minors under the law,[23] their appearance as defendants in trial can be expected to be governed by rules similar to those which regulate the procedure in reference to minors. Thus canon 1649 rules that collegiate and non-collegiate moral or legal persons are to be represented in court by the rector or administrator, except in the special causes mentioned in canon 1653. If the rights of the legal person conflict with those of the rector or administrator, the ordinary shall designate a procurator to represent the legal person.

When therefore the law says that the summons is to be served upon the one designated to act in the place of him who lacks procedural capacity, it means in the present context that the rector, the administrator or the procurator appointed by the ordinary is to be served with the summons.

Immediately, therefore, it seems that in the citation of a college, for example, the summons should read: "N.N., the rector or administrator of the college . . . as legal representative[24] is hereby cited" instead of the simple designation "the College of N.N. is hereby cited." On the other hand, it may be argued from the old law[25] that a summons worded in general terms is allowable when it is a university or a town, etc., that is being cited.

---

[22]Roberti, *De Processibus,* I, n. 291, p. 438; Wernz-Vidal, Vol. XI, n. 386, p. 332.

[23]Canon 100, § 3.

[24]Canons 1713, 1649.

[25]Pirhing, Lib. II, tit. 2, n. 217.

The present law in canon 1713 does not necessarily exclude the older interpretation. A closer look reveals that it states only the requirement that the summons be served on the legal representative and does not rule on the content of that summons. Since the law already makes clear the obligation of the rector to answer in trial in place of the college,[26] a summons citing the college as a defendant in a trial seems sufficient notification to the rector to appear.[27]

It is easy enough to envision how this could occur in practice. A letter, for instance, simply addressed to the college would be opened by the rector or referred to him, and he would then have ample notification, by reason of the enclosed summons, of the suit in which the college is named defendant, and that he under the law would be obliged to appear. In actual practice, of course, it would be preferable to indicate specifically the person being summoned in place of the moral person, and thus avoid ambiguity and forestall the raising of an exception. At least this much is certain, that the moral person must be properly designated and clearly indicated, or the summons will lack validity.

Canon 1650 is to be treated in any consideration extending to those who must be cited in place of the legally incapacitated. It expresses the rule that persons who because of their spendthrift habits have been deprived of the administration of their goods, and also the weak-minded,[28] can appear personally in court only

---

[26]Canon 1649.

[27]The Rota in an appeal hearing, *Froberger versus the Editors of Petrusblatter,* decided that the summons was null and void because it had not been directed to a specified person. The court which heard the cause in its first instance had addressed the summons to the editors in a general way.—*AAS,* Vol. V, (1913), p. 285. This does not seem to militate against the above mentioned opinion, for the editors, unlike a college, did not constitute a moral person and therefore lacked a representative already legally designated and under obligation to represent them.

[28]Krol, citing Coronata and Roberti, states that the judge may, but is not obliged to, follow the judgment of the civil authority relative to prodigality or mental debility of the litigants.—*Op. cit.,* p. 70. The Code Commission was asked: Whether, in virtue of canon 1651, § 1, in order to appoint a guardian for persons who are deprived of the use of reason or who are weak-minded, a regular judgment is necessary, or whether a decree of the ordinary, given after he has prudently investigated the matter, is sufficient. Reply: In the

to answer for their own offenses or at the order of the judge; otherwise they must sue and be sued through their guardians.

In this regard canon 1713 is to be applied in the following way. In those instances when the prodigal may appear personally in court, the summons may be served on him directly. There seem to be no reasons barring this mode of proceeding. In all other causes, however, his guardian should be cited. As regards the weak-minded, the summons should always be served upon the guardian, even in those causes wherein the weak-minded person may answer personally (if he is able) for his crime. In the same way no distinction was made by the Pontifical Commission for the Authentic Interpretation of the Code. It was asked whether the notice of the summons . . . should be sent by the person himself who is either deprived of the use of reason or weak-minded, or to the lawfully appointed guardian of the same. The Reply: In the negative to the first part, in the affirmative to the second.[29] Since the Commission made no distinction, it is correct to hold that the rule stated in the reply applies to all cases in which a weak-minded individual is involved, even in those in which he is allowed by the law to answer personally. The summons is to be served upon the guardian, who is to be advised of the court order for the weak-minded person himself to appear in court.

In turning to the question of a religious person being cited as defendant, one must bear in mind that no one can be called upon to answer for an action of which legally he is incapable. The one seeking redress must look beyond the individual to the

---

negative to the first part, in the affirmative to the second.—Pont. Com. Jan. 25, 1943 as reported in *AAS,* Vol. 35, p. 58. The question might further be asked with reference to the Commission's reply: Is the ordinary empowered to give a judgment, by decree, upon the mental capacity of a person or is it rather that he is empowered to effect, by decree, the appointment of a guardian? The reply seems to be principally concerned with the appointment itself; but this act of appointment, as considered in the Reply, does not seem to be divorced from a consideration of the states of those for whom the guardian is being appointed because an investigation is required. This seems to point to an investigation of the mental debility or the prodigality of the individuals concerned.

[29]Bouscaren, *Canon Law Digest,* Vol. III, pp. 603-604.

authority having the responsibility. Thus a judge is well advised to inform himself by preliminary investigation whether a religious person in a given cause acted with or without authorization.[30] If a religious, however, even a member of a regular Order, is legitimately constituted as rector or administrator of some moral person, such as a church or a benefice, the protection of whose rights does not depend on the religious superior, he may stand in judgment either as plaintiff or as defendant, and he does not need the special permission of the religious superior. This permission is implicit in the original assignment to the benefice or church or is consequent of a higher right given with the benefice. When the religious thus acts as defendant, he is not acting in his own name, as a private person, but in the name of the church or the benefice. Actually it is the moral person which acts as plaintiff or responds as defendant through him.[31]

Lega-Bartoccetti[32] say that not only religious professed with solemn vows but also religious with simple vows are embraced in the ruling of canon 1652. They hold that no distinction is to be made since the law itself makes no distinction. Following these remarks they very succinctly state the law thus: "*. . . quamobrem actionem non habet ex qua in iudicio agat, nec rem aut obligationem de qua ipse respondeat.*" Because of the impossibility adequately to cover the subject here, it can be stated in principle that the judge must inform himself whether

---

30Wernz-Vidal, VI, p. 173; Lega-Bartoccetti, Vol. I, p. 312. Wernz-Vidal, *ibid.*, in footnote n. 27 state the reasons why a religious person has not the right to stand in judgment; Ratio autem generalis regulae est, quia religiosus caret propriis bonis, saltem si sit professus, neque ullum habet ius in bonum, quod ipse personaliter possit actione persequi; sed quidquid acquirit monachus, monasterio acquirit et ideo monasterium potest vel debet agere, non monachus. Si vero agatur de contractibus, quae non respiciunt bona temporalia sed obligationes personales, quia religiosi proprium velle et nolle non habent, ideo *firmiter* absque *consensu* sui superioris sese obligare non possunt. Quare si Superior illum consensum denegaverit, *firma* non fuit obligatio religiosi, ac proinde nulla actio ex illa oriri potuit. At cum consensu Superioris religiosus pacta inire potest; quo in casu in altera parte oritur ius *agendi contra* talem religiosum ob pactum non servatum coram iudice competente.

31Wernz-Vidal, VI, p. 174.

32*Commentarius in Iudicia Ecclesiastica,* Vol. I, p. 313.

the individual religious acted illegitimately or as the duly constituted representative of the moral person, and therefore whether the summons is to be served upon him[33] or upon the superior of the community. As long as the religious acts as the agent of the community, it is the community itself that is to be summoned in litigation that may arise from that action of the religious. If the religious acts as a private individual, the community can disclaim responsibility and the individual himself is to be summoned when litigation concerns his private acts.

All holders of benefices can sue or be sued in the name of their benefices, but to act licitly they must observe the norm of canon 1526.[34] In such causes the summons would properly be served upon the holder of the benefice. Prelates and superiors of chapters, sodalities and of any other college cannot act in court in the name of their community unless they have obtained its consent in the manner defined by its statutes.[35] In the event that action is brought against such a group, the summons is served upon it as upon a moral person, if it has been juridically so constituted.

Finally canon 1654 states that *excommunicati vitandi* and also the *tolerati* after a declaratory or condemnatory sentence may personally institute an action in court for the purpose of attacking the justice or the legality of their excommunication; through a procurator, they may act in court to avert any other spiritual harm. . . . Other excommunicated persons are generally admitted to act in court. This canon regulates the possibilities granted by the law to excommunicated persons in their capacity

---

[33]When a member of a regular Order with the permission of his superiors has contracted debts and obligations, then the corporate entity whose superior has given the permission bears the responsibility; if the person is a religious with simple vows, he himself is responsible, unless he acted with the permission of the superior on behalf of the institute. If a religious contracts debts and obligations without any permission of his superiors, he himself is responsible, but not the institute, the province or the house.

In every cause, it is a rule that an action can always be brought against him for whom the contract has been a source of profit.—Canon 536, § 2, 3 and 4.

[34]Canon 1653, § 2.

[35]Canon 1653, § 3.

of plaintiff. Hence Lega-Bartoccetti[36] say that the common law in the causes considered in this canon does not prohibit the *vitandus* or the *toleratus* after a declaratory or condemnatory sentence from appearing personally as a defendant. They add, however, that the judge *ex officio* can require that they as defendants respond through procurators, if the public good demands this. Hence it will be left somewhat to the discretion of the judge to decide whether the summons is to be served upon the excommunicated party *(vitandus* or *toleratus)* or upon a duly constituted procurator.

Section 3. *Number of Persons to be Cited*

In the question of who can be cited one must advert to still another consideration, that of possessory trials.[37] These are to be conducted upon a summoning of only the adverse party, if the trial is instituted for the purpose of retaining or regaining possession. If there is question of the acquisition of possession (which the plaintiff never had), all who are interested in the matter are to be summoned. This is briefly illustrated by a Spanish author,[38] who stated that all are to be cited who believe that they have an interest or a right in something, as, for example, when through the newspapers all those are cited who believe that they can make claims in the settlement of a will or a pious legacy, etc.

Finally, as regards the defendant, the Code states that if there are several defendants each is to be summoned singly. This follows the rule governing the procedure of the Sacred Roman Rota,[39] namely that there should be made as many copies of the

---

[36]*Op. cit.,* Vol. I, p. 330.

[37]Canon 1700.

[38]*"Por la primera se llama a una persona o personas determinadas; pero por la general a todos los que se crean interesados o con derecho a una cosa, como cuando se llaman por los periodicos oficiales, o por edictos, a todos los que se crean con derecho a una testamentaria, legados piadosos etc. . . ."*— Franciscus Gomez de Salazar and Vincentius de la Fuente, *Tratado de Procedimientos Eclesiasticos,* (4 vols., Madrid, 1868), Vol. II, p. 326.

[39]Regulae Rotae, § 19, n. 2: *Deinde tot exemplaria citationis fiunt, et haec omnia Tribunalis Notarii subscriptione munita, quot sunt personae in ius*

summons as there are persons to be summoned. A corresponding notation should also be made on the copy reserved with the acts of the cause. This notation should relate the number of citations served.

Section 4. *Notice to the Plaintiff*

Finally, canon 1712 in its third paragraph states that the plaintiff must be notified by the court to appear on a specified day and at a fixed hour before the judge. The law in this particular canon is not clear as to the reason for the plaintiff's appearance in court. It could be for the joinder of issue, but it is not necessarily so, for the simultaneous presence in the court of the plaintiff and the defendant for the joinder of issue is not always required by law.[40] In such instances wherein it is required[41] the notification to the plaintiff to appear will be for the purpose of the joinder of issue. Otherwise it may be for the purpose of interrogation that the plaintiff is notified to appear. Whatever the case Noone[42] is surely correct in saying that an informal notice suffices for this notification of the plaintiff, since the Code has made no rules to govern the form it is to take, as well as in stating that no sanction of nullity becomes effective in case of violation of the rules governing this notification. If, however, the plaintiff is to be declared contumacious at any time, a formal summons is necessary.[43]

Article IV. Methods of Service

In brief it can be stated that Canon Law employs various methods in the service of the summons. In accordance with the

---

vocandae. In textu autographo ad calcem adnotabitur numerus exemplarius quae tradita fuerunt.—Fontes 6461. On the seventh of September, 1909, a set of norms drawn up by the judges of the Rota were presented to the Holy Father, Saint Pius X, for approbation, which he granted *ad experimentum.* Then on the second of August in the following year his final approbation was given and these norms had the force of law regulating the proceedings of the S. R. Rota.

[40] Canon 1727.

[41] Canon 1728.

[42] *Nullity in Judicial Acts,* p. 93.

[43] Canons 1849, 1724; Roberti, *De Processibus,* Vol. II, n. 410.

multiple variations that can arise in practice, the Code furnishes rules that outline in some detail the procedure to be followed. The summons is to be served either by a court messenger, or through use of the registered mail, or by way of edict, i.e., the publication of the summons in the papers or the posting of it in a public place. Particular rules govern and determine the selection of the method to be used in the service of the summons.

Section 1. *The Court Messenger*

Canon 1591 establishes the rule that couriers or messengers shall be constituted, either for all trials generally or for an individual cause, in order that they may serve notice of judicial acts, unless the approved custom of the tribunal dispenses with these officials. Apparitors (constables) should be appointed for the purpose of executing the sentences and decrees of the judge at his command.[44] One can feel safe in reflecting the opinion that many tribunals do not have permanently appointed couriers or messengers, so that other approved methods of communicating judicial acts to the ones concerned are *de facto* employed.

At any rate, the law in canon 1717, § 1, reads: "If it be possible, the summons is to be served upon the party, wherever he may be, by the court messenger." Strictly taken, this means that the service of the summons must be carried out by the court messenger, whenever possible, if it is to be done legitimately in the sense of canon 1723. In other words, the use of some other means, when it is possible to have service of the summons effected by the court messenger, would mean that the service of the summons is not legitimate. The use of the mail, for example, is a substitute method contingent upon the presence of a circumstance such as distance or some other special consideration which would render difficult the messenger's task of serving the summons.[45] If these circumstances are not present, it could seem

[44] These may be selected from members of the laity unless prudence would demand that an ecclesiastic be chosen for some specific cause at trial.—Canon 1592. *Cursores* and *apparitores* are variously designated in English: constables, bailiffs, beadles, marshals, sheriffs. Their attestation to the performance of their office is given full faith and credit.—Canon 1593.

[45] Canon 1719.

that the conditions which support the use of this method as legitimate are not verified.

On the other hand, it seems that this interpretation in all its strictness is not to be applied to the practice in this country. In many instances in virtue of canon 1591, the offices of court messenger and apparitor have been dispensed with, and by approved custom the substitution for these offices consists in the use of the mails. Therefore the rule of canon 1717 could not be urged, since this canon presupposes the existence or the presence on the staff of the tribunal of duly appointed messengers. Thus invalidity should not be predicated as following upon an illegitimate service of the summons, when, for example, the citation of a party, who could have been cited by court messenger had one been available, was sent by mail.

It is understandable that historically the service of the summons by means of the courier was of greater necessity. In fact it was usual for him to read the content of the citation, even though he might later post it in a public place.[46] In general, Canon Law adopted Civil Law in this matter. If the party could be found, he was to be cited personally; otherwise, at his home or at the place of his usual residence,[47] so that his procurator, if he left one, his servants or his friends might receive the summons for him.[48] Although now more clearly defined, these ideas figure in the present law.

In the actual service of the summons by the court messenger he is to proceed in the following manner. After the command or decree by which the judge orders the service of the summons has been given, the messenger is to act immediately.[49] Two copies of the citation are drawn up, one for the party being cited, the other for its preservation in the acts.[50] The rules for the pro-

[46] "We command ordinary judges to cite every absent litigant party by means not only of a call issued by messengers but also of a notice issued with edicts."—*Novellae* 112.

[47] D. (43.24) (5.2).

[48] Pirhing, Lib. II, tit. 2, n. 97; Lega, Vol. I, Lib. I, p. 431.

[49] Normae S. Romanae Rotae Tribunalis as issued on June 29, 1934.—Cf. *AAS*, XXVI (1934), 467.

[50] Canon 1716.

cedure followed in the S. R. Rota specify that the original is to be preserved in the acts, and only a copy served upon the party.[51] There is nothing, however, to indicate that this must be followed in the ordinary procedure of a diocesan tribunal. It makes little difference which copy is served upon the party being summoned, as long as it is properly composed and authenticated with the seal and the requisite signatures.

This summons is to be served upon the party himself. Although the law itself offers no suggestion regarding the ascertainment of the fact, it certainly includes the idea that the party upon whom the summons is served be sufficiently identified as the person specified in the citation. Obviously this must be done if the summons is to have its desired effect. Certainly if the messenger is to attest to the fact that the defendant has been duly cited, he must have knowledge of the identity of the person upon whom he served the summons. Although no such provision was made in the Code, there is evidence that one of the members responsible for the codification thought it desirable that he who received the summons sign it together with the messenger.[52] Perhaps he considered that a means of being apprised of the identity of the party summoned. In any case the procedure to be followed in the very act of serving the summons is outlined in canon 1721, §§ 1 and 2. When the messenger leaves the written summons in the hands of the defendant, he must sign it, marking the date and the hour at which he handed it to the defendant. He is to act in the same manner when he leaves the summons with a member of the family or a servant of the defendant, adding also the name of the person with whom he leaves the summons. If the summons is effected by means of a public notice, the messenger is to indicate, at the bottom of the notice, the day and the hour at which he posted the paper at the door of the curia, and how long it remained posted. If the defendant refuses to accept the summons offered him by the messenger, the latter is to mark the day and the hour, sign the summons, and then return it to the judge. Should there be

---

[51]Regulae, § 19, n. 1.—*Fontes*, N. 6461.

[52]Cf. footnote to Schema B, canon 206.—Roberti, *Schemata*, pp. 210-211.

any doubt about which copy is to be signed by the court messenger, it can be cleared up by means of a rule enacted for the S. R. Rota with reference to the same purpose that is served by the law of the Code. The Rotal rule is that the messenger is to note on both copies, the one for the acts and the one being served upon the party, the date, the name of the person accepting the summons, and his address together with his own signature.

Finally, the first paragraph of canon 1717 states that the court messenger is to serve the summons upon the party wherever he may be found. This was not always clearly the rule. A brief review of the earlier law as found in the Decretals[53] shows that authors were agreed on the law that an official *(praeses)* of one territory could not arrest *(realiter citare)* a delinquent found in another's jurisdiction. Rather, the citing official had to request the authority of the jurisdiction, wherein the defendant was found, to make the arrest and to hand over the defendant. Regarding the service of a verbal summons in the jurisdiction of another for a cause in which one was competently sitting in judgment there was disagreement. The glossator on the Decretal law just cited[54] presented arguments for both sides, and then stated that the doctors of canon law would not allow one to serve a summons, real or verbal, outside his territory. Instead he was to request a judge of the other jurisdiction to cite the party for him. Later on Lega (1860-1935) [55] subscribed to the opinions of De Luca (1614-1683) and Schmalzgrueber (1663-1735) in saying that the verbal citation could be served by the court messenger in another diocese, for the reason simply that such an act was not to be considered an act of jurisdiction. Theoretically he called this a *sententia tutissima,* but for practice he suggested that the courier should not be sent into another diocese to serve a summons. He thought it would be better to request through remissorial letters to a judge of the other diocese that he effect the service of the summons through one of his messengers.

A definitive settlement of the foregoing discussion has been

[53]C. 2, *de sententia et re iudicata,* II, 11, In Clem.

[54]*Glossa* ad c. 2, *de sententia et re iudicata,* II, 11, in Clem.

[55]*Praelectiones de Iudiciis Ecclesiasticis,* Vol. I, Lib. I, p. 434.

given in the Code. Canon 1717, § 2, reads: "The messenger may for this purpose (to serve the summons on the party wherever he may be found) enter the territory of another diocese, if the judge thinks it advisable and orders the messenger to do so." That this action by the courier or messenger is not an act of jurisdiction becomes clear when the prescription of this canon is considered in conjunction with canon 201. That canon states that one cannot exercise judicial power outside his own jurisdiction. Therefore the very fact that the courier is allowed by the law to serve the summons outside the jurisdiction of the citing judge shows his action to be only of a ministerial nature. It is explicit in the law, however, that the court messenger may not act in this way without authorization from the judge. Were he to serve the summons in another diocese without being commissioned to do so by the judge, the courier would act invalidly, for the illegality of his action would involve the invalidity mentioned in canon 1723. On this point it should not be argued that the courier is empowered, by virtue of the phrase *ubicumque is invenitur,* to serve the summons in another diocese by his own authority without the mandate from the judge. Against its historical background that phrase is to be understood as a settlement of the question whether the courier could even be sent into another diocese to serve the summons. The question revolved around the authority of the judge himself to send the courier, not around any problem of authority on the part of the courier himself. He was not even considered in this connection. When, therefore, the present law reads *"ubicumque is invenitur"* it is settling a question about the judge's authority, not that of the courier. The latter's power in this regard, i.e., serving the summons in another diocese, is determined in the second paragraph of canon 1717. He must await the mandate of the judge before he can act.

In this context—the service of the summons in another diocese—canon 1570, § 2, may be considered, since it contains the ruling that every tribunal has the right to call upon another tribunal for the examination or summons of the parties and the witnesses. This is known as the rogatory commission. Its use for the service of the summons in another diocese will depend upon the discretion of the judge ordering the citation. When used it would mean that the citing judge of Diocese A, where the case is being heard, would request the tribunal of Diocese B, where the defendant lives, to have the enclosed summons served upon the party by a courier of Diocese B. Regarding this method Roberti[56] makes the statement that it is rarely used. Nonetheless it is certainly a method that can be used at the discretion of the citing judge in virtue both of canon 1719 and of canon 1570. This follows the sense of a ruling that governed the procedure of the S. R. Rota.[57] In a given case the judge may decide that the use of a rogatory commission would be the safest way in which to effect the citation of the party who resides in another diocese.

In the final paragraph of canon 1717 is the rule: "If the messenger does not find the defendant in the place of his residence, he can leave the written summons with some person of the family or with a servant of the defendant, if that person is willing to accept the summons and promises to give it to the defendant as soon as possible; otherwise, the messenger shall take it back to the judge in order that he may dispatch it in the manner provided in canons 1719 and 1720.

A discussion arises concerning the list of persons with whom the courier may leave the summons, if he does not find the defendant at home. Is the list an all-inclusive one, so that all other persons are excluded, or is it simply demonstrative, so that others

---

[56] *De Processibus*, I, n. 294.

[57] Quoties pars in iudicium vocata neque suum procuratorem habeat, neque in Urbe commoretur; et ad eius commorationis locum facile non sit aut opportunum mittere tribunalis cursorem, citatio per officium tabellariorum remittetur Curiae ab Officiali distributore, ut eandem, *servatis servandis*, parti conventae transmittat. Transmissionis epistola *commendanda* est, et fides factae expeditionis asservanda in actis: id autem observari debet sive epistola ex officio, sive ad instantiam partis transmittatur.—Verum Ponens pro suo arbitrio permittere vel iubere potest ut non ope Curiae sed directe epistolam officialis distributor remittat parti conventae per officium publicum tabellariorum cauto tamen quod in actis constat de facta traditione; et hoc obtinetur per schedulam quae traditionem testetur factam, quaeque italice vocatur: *ricevuta de ritorno* (return receipt). *Regulae,* 24, n. 3.—Fontes, 6461. The older rule, although somewhat summarily stated in the new regulations of 1934, substantially remains in force by virtue of the new law.—*AAS,* Vol. 26, p. 467.

are in fact included? Lega-Bartoccetti[58] are of the opinion that the canon gives only an exemplary listing of the possible courses the messenger may pursue when he is unable to locate the defendant personally. In view of that opinion they say that the neighbors, if they meet the set requirements of the law, are included with members of the family and servants. Their reason is that the canon is chiefly concerned with the qualifications requisite in those who may be entrusted with the summons, namely their ability and willingness to see that it is delivered to the defendant. This, they say, can easily be verified in neighbors. Noone in his dissertation[59] takes exception to their opinion because of the fact that the canon allows the courier no discretionary power, but clearly states that, when he cannot consign the summons to the defendant or to a member of his family or to a servant of his household, he must return it to the judge. He cites several canonists who agree with this interpretation.[60] Although the reasoning by Lega-Bartoccetti seems plausible, one sees the value of Noone's interpretation enhanced by the fact that there was excluded from the final wording of the canon the proposal in the preliminary drafts of the Code to make it allowable to leave the summons with the neighbors when the defendant is not home.[61] Therefore it seems that the list of the canon is not to be extended to include the defendant's neighbors as suitable in law to receive the summons for him in his absence.

Those whom the Code lists as recipients of the summons in case the defendant is not home must meet certain qualifications stated in the law. They must be willing to accept the summons and promise to deliver it to the defendant as soon as possible. It is taken for granted here that they have sufficient mental capacity to be able later to testify, if need be, to the fact of the service of the summons on the defendant. Only if the requisite

---

[58]*Commentarius in Iudicia Ecclesiastica,* Vol. II, pp. 532-533.

[59]*Nullity in Judicial Acts,* p. 89.

[60]Coronata, *Institutiones,* III, n. 1245, p. 152; Wernz-Vidal, VI, p. 335; Prummer, *Manuale Iuris Canonici* (6 ed., Friburgi Brisgoniae: Herder, 1933), p. 582.

[61]Cf. Roberti, *Schemata,* F. can. 185, § 4, nota n. 13, pp. 211-212.

conditions are verified[62] can the courier leave the summons with these individuals. If he acts otherwise, he acts invalidly. Although not expressed in the law, the idea is implicit and the rule can be urged that service of the summons at the defendant's home, when no one is present, is an invalid act, i.e., the messenger can't just leave it in the mail box or tack it to the front door.

Canon 1718 states that the defendant who refuses to accept the citation is considered to be legitimately summoned. If, therefore, the courier returns to the judge a report that the defendant refused to accept the summons, the judge may pronounce contumacy, if he believes that the postulates of canon 1843 are satisfied, and proceed with the case. In this regard Roberti says that the defendant is to be considered cited when the summons is placed in his hands, whether he opens it or not. He cites a decision of the Signatura, which upheld the validity of a citation even though the defendant had not opened and read the letter.[63] The reason for this law is easily enough understood when one considers that the defendant could otherwise block the proceedings by way of his refusal. If the defendant within his legal rights could refuse the citation and not be considered legitimately cited, he could not be declared contumacious and would have at his disposal a means wherewith he could hinder the judicial settlement of a cause brought against him. That the law should be reduced to such a state that it could be rendered useless by the whim of an individual is an absurdity that cannot be subscribed to. Thus it is that the law considers as legitimately cited anyone who refuses to accept the summons legitimately served upon him.

Section 2. *Service through the Mails*

If for reasons of distance or in view of some other consideration it is difficult to have the summons delivered to the defendant by messenger, the judge can order it to be transmitted by registered mail with the request for a return receipt, or in any other manner which according to the laws and conditions

---

[62]This argument is drawn from the principle of canon 39.

[63]*De Processibus,* I, p. 442.

of the respective country is considered safest.[64] Since the use of this method by virtue of the law itself hinges upon the order of the judge[65] it can be said that its use in practice is left to his discretion. It is true that the law determines one reason for which this method may be used, that is, the factor of distance; still, that is only a general determination, so that in practice it will be the judge acting according to his discretion who will decide that the distance involved is such as to warrant the use of the mail. The same interpretation is applicable to that other general determination which speaks of a reason that would make it difficult for the summons to be served by the courier. In practice this also would be decided upon by the judge. The law does not specify what the difficulty might be nor does it identify the reason. It does not seem to be stretching the meaning of the law to have it include for example a situation in which the tribunal is understaffed and only with difficulty could have the summons served by a courier.

The requirement of the law that a return receipt be obtained must be complied with for the validity of this type of service. That is the force of the *dummodo* clause, argued from the interpretation elsewhere put on this word[66] as well as from the fact that this receipt will be the only way for the court to know that the summons has been served upon the party.

If the mails are not to be used for the service of the summons, the judge is to decide upon some other method. This too is allowed him in the law, and from the parallel place is occupies in the canon it seems to be an alternate method, and not simply a substitute for the use of the mails. Coronata[67] suggests as examples the use of a secular court messenger, the use of the rogatory commission, or the services of the pastor. This law had its origin in a pre-Code Instruction given by the Congregation for Bishops and Regulars in the year 1880. While ruling that the service of the summons should be effected by the court

---

[64]Canon 1719.

[65]. . . *vel praesidis in tribunali collegiali.*—Beste, p. 812; Article 80 of the Instruction *Provida.*

[66]Canon 39.

[67]*Institutiones,* III, n. 1246, p. 153.

messenger, it stated that some other method equally safe was allowable.[68]

Section 3. *Edictal Citation*

Gregory IX stated a reason warranting the use of the public, i.e., the edictal citation, in words which still have validity: *volentes finem impone litibus, ne immortales existant* . . .[69] Lega[70] in summary fashion spoke of the practice of the edictal citation. He said that ordinarily an individual was to be cited personally, but, if this could not be done, an edictal citation was to be used wherewith the defendant could be informed of the summons through his servants, neighbors or friends.[71] Another method for service of the edictal citation, when no one was to be found at the home of the defendant, was to post the written summons in a public place, to read it in church, or to publish it in the papers. Lega attested to the fact that this last method was one admitted by the S. Congregation of the Council (Jan. 23, 1875) for summoning individuals residing in far distant places.

In an earlier day, Reiffenstuel[72] while speaking of the edictal citation had described it as that which is affixed to the doors of churches, of the curia, or in some public place. More particularly notable, however, is the fact that he emphasized that it was to be used only in special circumstances. Some of these, delineated in the Decretal law, obtained: 1) when the party maliciously absented himself or otherwise impeded the citation from reaching him; 2) when the place in which the summons was to be served was not safe; 3) when the party was a vagabond . . . did not have a fixed domicile; and 4) if the defendant was not known for certain. In this last mentioned circumstance a general citation to all interested persons was posted. To these conditions Verano added the general one that the edictal citation

---

[68]*Fontes*, n. 2005.

[69]C. 10, X, *de dolo et contumacia*, II, 14.

[70]*Praelectiones in Iudiciis Ecclesiasticis*, Vol. I, Lib. I, p. 431.

[71]As the source for the practice of leaving the summons at the defendant's residence, although the defendant himself was not present, Lega cited c. 11, X, *de clericis non residentibus*, III, 4, and c. 10, X, *de dolo et contumicia*, II, 14.

[72]*Ius Canonicum Universum*, Lib. II, title 3, n. 76.

could be used when no other means could be found for citing an individual, for it remained the primary concern that the summons reach him.[73]

If one go beyond Lega and Reiffenstuel to the Decretal law, which they cited, one can note that Boniface VIII in speaking about the edictal citation stated that he was commanding nothing new in his rule that one who had placed obstacles to prevent a citation from reaching him was bound by the edictal citation, and could be considered contumacious for failure to comply. According to the Pope, the edictal citation in the situation just mentioned as well as in the situation when it was unsafe to approach the domicile of the one being cited was to be affixed to the door of the curia, and after a reasonable length of time the party was to be considered summoned the same as if it had been personally served upon him.

Clement V, in commenting on Boniface's law, remarked that those stringent measures were necessitated by reason of the malicious conduct on the part of many during those times. He added, however, that he was mitigating the rigor of Boniface's law, so that the full effect of the edictal citation equivalent in the law to the personal summons, would assert itself solely against those who had in some way impeded the citation.

Thus the edictal citation in the law today bears similarity to the earlier law, at least substantially and in its effect. The most notable difference lies in the statement of the reasons which allow its use. The old law, i.e., the Decretal law, called for the edictal citation when the defendant placed obstacles to a personal service of the summons. When this occurs under the Code law, and is sufficiently established, the defendant can be considered as legitimately cited, as has already been seen.[74] The condition, as stated in the present law, by reason of which a use of the edictal citation is authorized consists simply in this that the defendant cannot be found.

Canon 1720 gives the rule that the summons by edict can take place whenever after diligent inquiry it cannot be ascertained

[73]Vol. II, p. 273.

[74]Canon 1718.

where the defendant stays. The text makes it clear that this method is not to be used indiscriminately, but only after a diligent inquiry has been made concerning the whereabouts of the one to be summoned. To proceed to the use of the edictal citation before making any inquiry is to act without the authorization of the law, and such action would have no legal force because of the very fact that the law makes the judge's decision to use the edictal citation hinge upon the fact of an inquiry having been made. The judge's exercise of discretionary power applies only to the sufficiency of the inquiry and the fact of its negative result with reference to locating the one to be cited. Therefore, it is necessary for the legitimate use of this method of serving the summons, that the inquiry be made. Moreover, since the validity of the summons as well as subsequent procedural acts hinges upon a legitimate service of the summons[75] the inquiry must be made before the edictal citation can validly be used.

The manner in which this summons is to be served is outlined in the law.[76] The messenger posts the document of the summons on the door of the curia in the manner of a public notice. This notice is to be left there for a length of time specified by the judge. The messenger likewise inserts the summons in some public newspaper. Either of these methods suffices if one or the other cannot be employed. Doheny[77] remarks that all possible means are to be used for the purpose of making this method effective when it is employed. He is surely stating the obvious when he says that a summons posted on the door of a chancery today would receive scant notice. Hence, he adds, the judge may well feel obliged in many instances to insert a citation by edict in the public newspaper, e.g., the diocesan paper.

According to the preliminary drafts of canon 1720,[78] it was at the cathedral church that the summons was to be posted, and it was in the Catholic papers that the summons was to be published. By the time of the final draft neither of these remained

[75]Canon 1723.

[76]Canon 1720, § 2.

[77]*Canonical Procedure in Matrimonial Cases,* Vol. I, p. 257.

[78]Roberti, *Schemata,* B, can. 92, pp. 214-215.

in the statement of the law and any public newspaper was considered a suitable means of publication of the summons. Doheny,[79] however, calls attention to the possibility of scandal or difficulty with the civil law, if these notices are published in the secular press. The judge would do well to be advised of any such possibility. In our country the Catholic papers will certainly be adequate for the purposes of a legitimate service of the edictal citation. The choice of the paper in which to have the summons published should be governed by a consideration of which paper will best serve the purpose of making it known.[80]

Article 4, Canon 1724

The rules governing the citation of the defendant are to be accommodated and applied to notices of other acts of the trial, such as the court orders and sentences of the judge, in keeping with their peculiar characteristics.

The notification spoken of in this law is well explained by Lega-Bartoccetti[81] as applicable to those acts which the judge either *ex officio* or at the instance of one of the parties orders to be served upon the other.[82]

In addition to a familiarity with the rules for the service of the summons one must, for the application of canon 1724, have a clear grasp of the other stages of the proceedings in a trial. Exemplifying the application of this canon are the citation of witnesses,[83] the publication of the process,[84] notification to the parties to present their briefs either personally or through their

---

[79]*Loc. cit.*

[80]Lega-Bartoccetti, *Commentarius in Iudicia Ecclesiastica,* II, 535; Wernz-Vidal, VI, n. 389.

[81]*Op. cit.,* Vol. III, p. 540.

[82]Lega-Bartoccetti *(loc. cit.)* speak of judicial acts as being of two classes: those which occur within the trial itself, e.g., the joinder of issue, depositions, and such acts which, though in existence before the trial, are submitted to the court as evidence in the trial. The former they say may be made known to the parties, so that a possible exception may be raised, the latter by a prescription of the law (canons 1859-1861) must be made known to the other party.

[83]Canon 1765.

[84]Canon 1859.

advocates,[85] and the citation to the parties to hear the sentence.[86] This is only a demonstrative listing of acts wherein notification to the individuals concerned will be made according to the rules of canon 1724.

The citation of witnesses, for example, is by reason of canon 1765 explicitly made subject to the rule of 1724. Canon 1765 states that the summoning of witnesses is to be done through the medium of the judge by whose decree the summons is served upon the witness in the manner prescribed in canons 1715-1723. Lega-Bartoccetti,[87] in saying that this summons is to be drawn up according to the rule of canon 1715, are simply presenting the obvious statement of the law. Since this citation of the witness is included in the phrase *ceteris quoque iudicii actibus,*[88] it is correct to assume that the content of the citation will be adapted to the summoning of a witness. In consideration of the requirements that the summons include a general statement regarding the cause, Lega-Bartoccetti[89] partially disagree with Noval[90] by saying that it would be allowable at times to include in the summons to a witness the points on which he is to be questioned. Lega-Bartoccetti are cognizant of the fact that this seems to conflict with the rules of canon 1776, which prohibits revelation to the witness of the forthcoming interrogatory to which he will be subjected. One can agree with them when they say that the points on which one is to be questioned are not to be identified with the interrogatory itself; and indeed they may at times be made known, within the law stated in canon 1776, if the judge believes that this can be done without prejudice to the testimony of the witness. If danger either of fraud or of collusion is present, only a general statement regarding the cause upon which the witness is to be questioned will be stated in the summons.

Since it is within the provisions of the law for the edictal

[85]Canon 1862.

[86]Canon 1877.

[87]*Op. cit.,* Vol. II, p. 692.

[88]Cf. canon 1724.

[89]*Op. cit.,* Vol. II, p. 692.

[90]*De Processibus,* Vol. I, p. 288.

citation to be used in the summoning of witnesses, a certain qualification needs to be made. This arises from the law itself, since the very ignorance[91] which necessitates the edictal citation renders inadmissible the testimony of the witness whose domicile is unknown.[92] This inadmissibility can be overruled, however, by the same law, if the judge deems this testimony necessary inasmuch as the proofs already collected still are insufficient. In the event, then, that the domicile of a witness is unknown, the use of the edictal citation will depend ultimately upon the judge's decision concerning the necessity of testimony from that witness.

Finally, concerning the summons to witnesses it is clear from canon 1765 that canon 1723 applies. If the law in this matter[93] be not observed, the summons is invalid, as are also whatever acts depend upon it.[94]

In the other examples given above, i.e., the publication of the process, notification to the parties to file their briefs, and the summons to hear the sentence, canon 1724 will be applied in the adaptation of the rules governing the initial summons. Naturally the cause will have to be identified, the purpose of the notice given, and the place and time stated, if appearance in the trial is being required. The rule is not a stringent one; it leaves its application in detail to the discretion of the judge who will accommodate to the various situations the rules on the summons. As long as those regulations are substantially observed, no invalidity will result.[95]

---

[91]Cf. canon 1720.

[92]Canon 1749.

[93]Canons 1715-1723 by reason of canon 1765; 1724.

[94]Cf. canon 1680, § 2.

[95]Noone, *Nullity in Judicial Acts*, p. 92.

CHAPTER IV

Effects of the Summons

All the foregoing about the content of the summons and its service upon the party has meaning ultimately in the effects produced. The primary result, namely the presence of the cited party in the trial, has already been mentioned together with the corresponding effect of contumacy when the summons is disobeyed.[1] These are almost self-evident in the very nature of the summons and come to light particularly in an examination of its content. Other effects which are stated explicitly in the law[2] are not immediately obvious, and conversely are to be examined from the approach of a positive statement of the law if one is to initiate a scrutiny of the underlying reasons.

These effects, now neatly expressed in the compactness of the Code, are not a schema arbitrarily formulated and imposed upon judicial practice; rather, as has most often happened, the present law is the formulated result of a progressive development occasioned by a diversity of situations. The effects of the summons, as now stated in the law, are not therefore the result of related efforts to produce a systematic legal practice, but are instead the crystallization of various principles unrelatedly enunciated at different times especially in the Decretal pronouncements.

Canon 1725 reads: When the defendant has been legitimately summoned, or the parties have of their own accord appeared in court, this act has the following effects: (1) the matter in litigation ceases to be a matter still intact *(res integra);* (2) the cause becomes proper to the judge or the court where the action has been instituted; (3) the jurisdiction of a delegated judge is rendered firm, so that it does not expire with the loss of jurisdiction of the one who delegated him; (4) the course of legal prescription suffers interruption, unless a contrary proviso

---

[1]Cf., *supra,* pp. 1, 30.

[2]Canon 1725.

obtain according to the norms of canon 1508; and (5) the litigation begins to hang in the balance, and accordingly the principle of law which immediately begins to apply is the following: *pending the litigation, nothing may be changed.*

The initial statement of this canon is, in short, an application of the law stated in the canons immediately preceding,[3] for the legitimate service of the summons means that it is done in accordance with those provisions. If this is not done, nullity results,[4] the basis for the effectual realization of canon 1725 is lacking, and the results therein listed do not follow. Wherefore the summons which is not legitimately executed has no juridical effect.[5] Thus is reiterated the necessity of care in this matter that the summons be drawn up according to the provisions of canon 1715, and served upon the party in one of the ways prescribed in the canons.[6] When all those rules are followed, that is, those which are applicable to a definite situation, the summons will have been legitimately executed and will produce the legal effects outlined by the law.

In a similar manner the spontaneous appearance of the parties for the trial, as stated in canon 1725, will produce the same result. This is the spontaneous appearance discussed earlier,[7] which must be verified before the juridical effect similar to that resulting from a legitimate summons will follow. The spontaneity in this regard is understood in a rather restricted sense, that of the act which is *simpliciter voluntarium.*[8] In other words, the party can be said to be spontaneously present, in the sense of canon 1725, when the reason for his appearance lies exclusively in his own initiative. This does not obtain if the party appears because he erroneously believes himself bound by a

[3]Canons 1711-1724.

[4]Canon 1723.

[5]Cf. Coronata, *Institutiones,* Vol. III, p. 155, citing Reiffenstuel, Lega, Wernz and others.

[6]Canons 1712, 1713, 1716-1722.

[7]Cf. Chapter I, pp. 7, 8; cf. also Wernz-Vidal, Vol. VI, n. 393, nota 48.

[8]Cf. Noldin-Schmidt, *Summa Theologiae Moralis,* 27 ed., 3 vols., Oeniponte/Lipsiae, Sumptis et Typis Feliciani Rauch, 1940-1941, Vol. I, *De Principiis,* p. 48, n. 42.

summons, which, however, is in fact illegal. The party's appearance in such circumstances would evince a modified voluntariness *(voluntarium secundum quid)* and would not be effective in healing the illegality of the summons, if he chose to raise an exception. If an individual knows of the defects of the summons, but nevertheless appears and lodges no exception, he is understood to be spontaneously present.

The question must here be raised with reference to the first requirement of canon 1725, more specifically with regard to the meaning of the phrase *legitime peracta.* Since the realization of the effects outlined in canon 1725, in all those instances when the parties do not spontaneously appear, hinges upon the accomplishment of this *legitimate execution* of the citation, it is necessary to know how this is accomplished before one can determine that the effects have followed. The one serviceable norm which is legally acceptable and readily available to determine the meaning of the phrase *legitime peracta* is the context in which canon 1725 is placed. This means that the answer to the question concerning the significance of a legitimate execution of the citation lies principally in those canons which treat of the elements requisite for a valid citation and in those which govern its legitimate service on the party. In view of the provisions therein stated the least that the phrase *legitimately executed* can signify is that the summons formulated according to the norms of the canons has actually been served in accord with the prescribed methods. According to this interpretation, it is not necessary to the accomplishment of a *legitimate execution* of the citation that it has actually reached the party. On the other hand the most that the phrase *legitime peracta* can signify is that the citation has been authoritatively and properly formulated, has been legally served upon the party, and that he has actually received it.

There is an historical basis for making this distinction as well as for accepting the first interpretation as applicable in the present Canon Law. The choice of the first interpretation, whereby the phrase *legitime peracta* is understood to include the formulation of the citation and its service upon the party exclusive of his actual coming into possession of the citation, rests upon the pre-Code determination of the time at which certain of the effects were realized subsequent to the service of the summons.[9]

Canon 1725 does not necessarily imply that each and every effect is to take place at precisely the same procedural moment following the legitimate execution of the citation. This opinion is expressed in view of pre-Code interpretation that the precise moment at which a given effect was realized was not the same for all the effects. In certain instances the legal effect of the citation was not realized until such time as the summons reached the cited party.[10]

What then is the meaning of those effects which follow from the fulfillment of the law initially stated in canon 1725? The first of the effects listed[11] is that the matter in litigation ceases to be a matter still intact, i.e., the cause is before the court, and the matter involved in the cause is no longer a private affair, but one in which the public authority is interested.

This effect takes place in all causes regardless of the nature of the matter in litigation. It is not to be thought that the term *res* of canon 1725, n. 1, refers only to real property, and that the matter in litigation ceases to be a *res integra* only in those causes which involve real property. Rather, the term *res* is to be understood to refer in general to whatever is the matter in controversy before the court. The reason for this interpretation is to be found in the canon considered by itself as well as in the context.

---

[9]Regarding the effect which is now listed as number 3 in canon 1725 Reiffenstuel stated: ". . . *per solam citationem a delegato, emissam quamvis nondum ante obitum delegantis ad notitiam citati pervenerit, jam perpetuari jurisdictionem delegati, Et merito: quia delegatus emittendo citationem, jam coepit uti sua jurisdictione; et consequenter censetur perpetuata sua jurisdictio.*"—Lib. II, tit. 3, n. 106.

[10]"Citatio a judice competenti emanata inducit litispendantiam, postquam tamen ad partem citatam pervenerit, vel per eam factum fuerit, quominus ad eius notitiam pervenerit. Textus est in Clem. 2. *ut lite pendente* etc., ubi proinde *glossa* s.v. *ad partem,* et Abbas n. 6 advertent, quod licet quoad perpetuandam jurisdictionem sufficiat emanasse citationem; sed ulterius requiratur, quod pervenerit ad partem citatam, per textum ibidem."—Reiffenstuel, Lib. II, tit. 3, n. 107.

[11]Canon 1725, n. 1.

Canon 1725 lists the effects that follow the summons legitimately issued or served, and it does this without any indication whatsoever that these effects are to follow only in certain types of causes. It follows therefore that the canon applies to all causes heard according to the formal procedure, unless its application is limited by the rule on the specific effect or by the nature of the effect. No such exception is evident in the rule on the first effect, nor is the nature of the effect such as to refer exclusively to real property. For this reason the term *res* is to be understood to refer to whatever constitutes the matter that is in litigation.

The fundamental law of canon 1725, n. 1, was well stated by Pope Gelasius I (492-496) in his application of it to a cause involving real property.[12] He was asked whether the plaintiff could demand some sort of pension from the object in litigation which the defendant held in his possession. The Pope's answer was in the negative, and he positively stated that the object was to remain in the hands of the defendant, who, however, would act invalidly if he did anything prejudicial to the interests of the other party before a settlement.[13] The substantial element considered here lies in the very nature of litigation, for the controverted object can well be thought of as juridically divided, inasmuch as two parties are claiming full ownership over the same object. Since each has only a partial claim before the law

[12]Quia res in litigio posita in nullam transferri potest omnino personam, donec legitimae cognitionis eventu, cui potius debeatur, iudiciaria disceptatione possit agnosci, ex eadem re quispiam non sinatur exigere pensiones, sed in eodem statu re eadem posita, in quo videtur ante constituta, quisquis sibi putat quippiam posse competere, iuridico pulset examine, preiudiciis omnibus inde submotis.—c. 50, C. XI, q. 1.

[13]*Glossa Ordinaria* ad c. 50, C. XI, q. 1. *casus.*

The basic element in this law was early recognized in legal systems. Under the formulary procedure of Roman Law, when an object was in litigation, it could be assigned by the praetor to one of the litigants, and this individual was then ordered to give to his adversary sureties both for the property and for the profits.—Sherman-Robinson, *Roman Law Readings* (2 vols., Baker Voorhis & Co., New York, 1933), Vol. I, p. 225.

Roman Law likewise made provision for a proper handling of the situation when an object in litigation was alienated either in good or in bad faith.—C. (8.36) 5.

in the very act of litigation, neither is to be allowed such action as would presuppose the full rights which are still to be determined by the litigation. These ideas, it can be said, are inherent in the very notion of litigation. Their effective realization at a stated moment, however, arises from the rule of positive law, and in this matter the positive law states that the object of litigation ceases to be a *res integra* once the summons is legitimately served. It does not seem that this effect takes place before the summons reaches the party who is being cited, for one should hardly be limited in one's actions with respect to a given object or right until one has been authoritatively apprised of the fact that the public authority has removed it, temporarily at least, from private determination.

The second effect of the legitimate summons is that the cause becomes proper to the judge or the court where the action has been instituted. This is the same rule as that given in canon 1568, which reads: by reason of prior option, when two or more judges are equally competent, that judge has the right to hear the cause who first issued the summons to the defendant and thus legitimately cited him to his tribunal.[14] Such a situation could occur when a cause can allowably be presented before any one of two or more tribunals in virtue of different grounds for competence, such as domicile, quasi-domicile, or contract.

The question could be raised: precisely at what moment does this effect take place: Is it at the time when the judge orders the summons, when he has it served, e.g., placed in the mails, or only after it has reached the cited party? Few authors treat the question. Reiffenstuel, among those who did, furnished a definite statement. His statement appears to represent the more reasonable view. He insisted that the service of the summons—once it had reached the cited party—so restricted him that he was bound to appear before the judge who had cited him, and was barred from taking this same cause to any other tribunals which before had been equally competent.[15] His opinion clearly indicated that this effect, namely the exclusion of other heretofore com-

---

[14]Cf. also canons 1558, § 2; 205, § 2.

[15]*Ius Canonicum Universum,* Lib. II, tit. 3, n. 104.

petent tribunals from hearing the cause, did not result until the summons had reached the party being cited. This opinion he undoubtedly derived from an examination of the Decretal Law.

Gregory IX (1227-1241) had spoken of a situation in which an individual moved to another jurisdiction and felt that he could decline to appear before the tribunal of his former residence, whereto he had been cited before his change of domicile.[16] This, according to Gregory, was not allowed. From his statement it is definitely clear that the jurisdiction of one court was established to the exclusion of others once the summons had reached the party being cited; however, he did not say whether or not this could be effected before that moment. The most that can be said is that this Decretal pronouncement, considered alone, is silent on the question whether the jurisdiction of the court is firmly established, and that of the others is excluded, by the service of the summons even before it reaches the party. This same silence is found in another instance of the Decretal legislation,[17] and in the light of Reiffenstuel's interpretation, that the citation must reach the party to accomplish the effect of prior option *(locus praeventionis),* it is reasonable to assert that the other interpretation, namely that the legally served summons produces this effect of prior option even before it reaches the cited party, is excluded. Therefore, in the present law, unchanged from that of the Decretals, the legally served summons must reach the party being cited before it will produce this second named effect (canon 1725, n. 2).

In the use of the edictal citation the determination of this fact, that the summons has reached the cited party, can hardly

---

[16]Proposuisti nobis quod quidam subditus tuus ad petitionem cuiusdam adversarii sui a te legitime citatus ad causam, quia postmodum iurisdictionis alterius esse coepit, tuum intendit iudicium declinare. Porro tuae prudentiae dubium esse non credimus, quod is in praedicta causa ius revocandi forum non habet, quasi ab altero iam praeventus.—c. 19, X, *de foro competente,* II, 2.

Another old principle applies here: *Ubi acceptum est semel iudicium, ibi et finem accipere debet.*—D. (5.1) 30.

[17]C. 7, X, *de appellationibus,* II, 28.

be established. Nevertheless, service of the summons in edictal fashion, in keeping with the traditional practice, renders possible pursuit of the trial independently of any knowledge that the summons has reached the cited party. In the situation when two competent tribunals summon a party by edictal citation, prior claim to hear the cause will rest with that tribunal which was first in publishing the summons.[18]

Thirdly, the legitimate summons or its legal equivalent has the effect that the jurisdiction of a delegated judge is rendered firm, so that it does not expire with the loss of jurisdiction of the one who delegated him.[19] The focal point of consideration in this particular provision of the law is the loss of power on the part of the delegator, and how this affects the power of the delegate in judicial matters. In the event that the delegating judge has lost his power or office, whether by natural or civil death,[20] the judge delegate may not proceed in a given cause, unless he has already legally executed the summons. When this has been done, the principle of the exceptional clause in the general law on the cessation of delegation goes into effect, which states that the delegation will end with the delegator's death, civil or natural, if the mandate so provides, unless the matter is no longer intact.[21]

The present law with regard to the effect of the legitimate summons in establishing the permanency of a delegate's power seems to vary a bit from the old law. Earlier legislation can be seen applied in a cause proposed to Pope Lucius III (1181-1185). This pope gave the following response to the Archbishop of Canterbury and his Suffragans: "Our consultatory response to you is as follows: If the joinder of issue took place before the death of Our Predecessor, the mandate in no way expired with the death of the mandator. However, if he died before the

[18]Canon 1568.

[19]Canon 1725, n. 3.

[20]Schmaltzgrueber, Lib. I, tit. 29, n. 45.

[21]Cf. Kearney, *The Principles of Delegation,* The Catholic University of America Canon Law Studies, n. 55 (Washington, D. C.: The Catholic University of America, 1929), p. 115.

joinder of issue, the judges whom he delegated must not proceed in virtue of such delegation."[22]

If one were to consider only the wording of that text, one could be led to state that there is an obvious difference between the old law and the new, and that the old law can offer little towards reaching exactitude in the interpretation of this new particular provision. On the other hand, the glossator's view[23] in conjunction with other instances of legislation[24] lent greater weight to the opinion that the new law does not differ from the old. Thus the teaching of a pre-Code author such as Reiffenstuel has more detailed pertinence for the understanding of the present law. Speaking in particular about the precise moment when this effect of the legitimate summons takes place, he stated that it is immaterial to the realization of this effect of establishing delegated jurisdiction whether or not the summons has actually reached the cited party before the death of the delegator. He added that once the delegate had seen to the legitimate service of the summons he has begun to employ his jurisdiction, and it is by that act established for that particular case.[25] Since the new law remains unchanged from the old, this interpretation is still valid and applies to the present law.

The fourth legal effect of the summons legitimately executed or its equivalent is stated in this way: the course of legal pre-

---

[22]C. 19, X, *de officio et potestate iudicis delegati*, I, 29.

[23]In his explanation the glossator stated that according to the canons it was not only the joinder of issue that was considered as establishing the continued existence of the delegated power, but that the citation also secured the same effect. It alone, if served before the death of the mandator, was sufficient to perpetuate the rescript of delegation. If the citation did not precede the death of the mandator the mandate ceased.—*Glossa Ordinaria,* ad c. 19, X. de officio et potestate iudicis delegati, I, 29, s.v., *contestata.*

[24]*Si delegatus citavit ante mortem delegantis, perpetuata est eius iurisdictio.* —c. 20, X, *de officio et potestate iudicis delegati,* I, 29; *Ad hoc: Quaedam causa fuit commissa iudici delegato, ipse statim citavit partes; lis vero contestata fuit post mortem delegantis; quaerebatur utrum possit postea in causa procedere delegatus. Respondit Papa quod citatione facta negotium est quasi coeptum et praecipue si delegatus non sit certus de obitu delegantis, unde legitime potest in causa procedere.*—Glossa ad c. 20, X. *de officio et potestate iudicis delegati,* I, 29, s.v. *casus.*

[25]*Ius Canonicum Universum,* Lib, II, tit. 3, n. 106.

scription suffers interruption unless a contrary proviso obtain according to the norm of canon 1508.[26] The text of this latter canon reads as follows: prescription, as a means of acquiring (property) and of freeing oneself (from an obligation) is admitted by the Church in regard to church property according to the civil legislation of each respective nation. However, all the reservations that are enacted in the Code must be observed.[27] According to its twofold effect prescription is divided into acquisitive and liberative. Both are governed immediately and in detail by the positive enactments of human law. If acquisitive prescription is to take effect, five conditions must generally be verified: 1) a thing that is prescriptible; 2) actual possession; 3) some kind of title; 4) the requisite lapse of time; and 5) good faith.[28]

The present law which effects an interruption in the course of legal prescription by way of the legitimate service of the summons, applies to both the acquisitive and liberative prescription mentioned in canon 1508, unless an exception appears.

The old law in this regard considered legal prescription under a three-fold division, and accordingly stated that the summons interrupted only the prescription *longissimi temporis.*[29] The new law (canon 1725) makes no like distinction and seems therefore to apply to all prescription considered in canon 1508. If the present law, namely that the legitimate summons interrupts the course of legal prescription is applicable to only a certain type, it should, like the old law, invoke a clear distinction. It does not do so, and therefore seems to apply to legal prescription in the completeness of the approach which canon 1508 appears

---

[26]Canon 1725, n. 4.

[27]Reference is made to canons 1509-1512.

[28]Bouscaren-Ellis, *Canon Law, A Text and Commentary* (2 ed., Milwaukee: The Bruce Publishing Company, 1951), p. 810.

For a thorough treatment of canon 1508 cf. Martin, *Adverse Possession, Prescription and Limitation of Actions. The Canonical "Praescriptio,"* The Catholic University of America Canon Law Studies, n. 202 (Washington, D. C.: The Catholic University of America Press, 1944).

[29]Cf. Reiffenstuel, Lib. II, tit. 3, n. 109; Lega-Bartoccetti, *Commentarius in Iudicia Ecclesiastica,* Vol. II, p. 543.

to make.[30] One can hardly argue from the rule of canon 6, n. 4, that the old law is to be adhered to; that would hardly apply here, for there is definitely a difference between the old and the new law on the types of prescription considered in this context. The old looked to a threefold division; the new, according to canon 1508, has adopted the variations of the various state laws, with uniformity only in the canonical exceptions. This variety or possibility of variety is hardly to be equated with the fixed division of the old law, and it does not seem reasonable to expect the rules of the old law, which hinged upon a clear division, to be applied to a variety that defies equal application.

In their discussions of the manner in which this effect of the summons takes place the authors are particularly considering acquisitive prescription. Coronata[31] is certainly correct in stating with others[32] that the effect of the interruption of prescription follows upon the legitimate summons, not by reason of the loss of the requisite good faith, which does not necessarily follow the citation, but by reason of the provision of the law. Were it true that this effect occurred by reason of the loss of good faith, it would be possible to have a cause in which, even after the summons, one would continue in good faith and prescription would not be interrupted. The law, however, does not seem to contemplate such a situation, and it does not distinguish by pointing to instances when this interruption of prescription by the legitimate summons will occur, and to others when it will not. It seems therefore to mean that this interruption of prescription occurs always after the serving of the legitimate summons apart from any consideration of the continued presence of good faith or its destruction thereby.

This effect of the legitimate summons seems to apply as well to prescription in criminal causes, even though no specific mention of these is included in canon 1508, to which canon 1725

[30]Cf. also canon 1701.

[31]*Institutiones*, Vol. III, p. 155.

[32]Wernz-Vidal, Ius Canonicum, Vol. VI, p. 338; *Interrumpitur: non quidem naturaliter, id est, ob defectum alicuius conditionis ad praescribendum, aut ob omissionem bonae fidei, sed civiliter seu ob praescriptum legis.*—Noval, *De Processibus*, Vol. I, p. 289.

points in its reference.[33] Canon 1712 implies that legal prescription has run its complete course whenever the time fixed by the law for entering a criminal action has expired. If criminal action is entered, however, then the time is interrupted and so is the prescription. One could hardly say that "criminal action" is entered against a person before the trial is begun, and, since that is commonly held to occur with the citation, it is by the same that prescription in criminal cases is interrupted.

The last of the effects of the legitimate summons named in the Code is that the litigation begins to hang in the balance and accordingly there immediately applies the principle of law: pending the litigation, nothing may be changed.[34] That is to say, that, pending the litigation, any innovations will be considered *attentata* and may be declared as such. Canon 1854 principally explains what such innovations might be. The prejudicial attempts there mentioned are prohibited while the cause is pending. To be designated as such acts are, for example, the attempted transferral of the possession of the object that is in litigation; the attempted alienation of the object;[35] or the petition for a rescript regarding the matter that is in litigation apart from all mention that a pertinent or related cause is pending.[36] In order that the case be considered to be pending it is necessary that the citation have reached the cited party.[37] At that moment this last named effect, barring all innovations once the case is pending, is realized.[38]

[33]Cf. also canon 1701.

[34] Canon 1725, n. 5.

[35]C. 3, X, ut lite pendente nihil innovetur, II, 16.

[36]Coronata, Institutiones, Vol. III, p. 156.

[37]Reiffenstuel, Lib. II, tit. 3, n. 107.

[38]Notetur quod quamquam ad perpetuandam iurisdictionem sufficiat citationem emanasse a iudice, licet non pervenerit ad partem, quoad inducendam litis pendentiam oportet quod pervenerit citatio ad partem.—*Glossa Ordinaria,* ad c. 2, *ut lite pendente nihil innovetur,* II, 5, in Clem.

CONCLUSIONS

1. The historical development of the summons *(vocatio in ius* —canon 1711, § 1), even apart from the positive statement of the law, is suggestive of the necessity of the summons for the validity of a judicial process.
2. As the summons is fundamentally necessary for the validity of a formal trial, so it is required also for the validity of the summary process (canon 1990).
3. In the application of the rules of the formal trial with reference to the citation to the summary process, modifications may be made as long as the summons, in content and service, substantially remains a summons.
4. The collegiate body, precisely for the reason that it is the *iudex* (canon 1712, § 1) in a certain case, is to issue the order calling for the summons to be served.
5. The text of the summons basically must always be expressive of a command; it is to be worded in such a way that it does not lose its preceptive character.
6. It is not an absolute requirement that the bill of complaint always be sent with the summons to the defendant; in some instances the general description of the case in the text of the summons will suffice.
7. The determination in the summons of the day on which the defendant must appear is left to the discretion of the judge hearing the case.
8. In virtue of canon 1591 the use of the mails for the service of the summons can be an approved substitute for the court messenger, even in the absence of such conditions as are ordinarily presupposed by the law for the use of the mails as a method of serving the summons.
9. For its validity the courier's service of the summons in another diocese must originate in a specific order of the citing judge.
10. The precise moment at which each effect of canon 1725 is realized is not the same for all the effects.

BIBLIOGRAPHY

Sources

Acta Apostolicae Sedis, Commentarium Officiale, Romae, 1909- .

Bouscaren, T. Lincoln, *The Canon Law Digest,* 3 vols. through 1953, Milwaukee: Bruce Publishing Co., Vol. I, 1934, Vol. II, 1943, Vol. III, 1954.

Codex iuris Canonici Pii X Pontificis Maximi iussu digestus, Benedicti Papae XV auctoritate promulgatus, Praefatione, Fontium Annotatione et Indice Analytico-Alphabetico ab Emo Petro Card. Gasparri Auctus, Romae: Typis Polyglottis Vaticanis, 1917; reimpressio, 1934.

Codicis Iuris Canonici Fontes, cura Emi Petri Card. Gasparri editi, 9 vols., Romae (postea Civitate Vaticana) ; Typis Polyglottis Vaticanis, 1923-1939. (Vols. VII-IX, ed cura et studio Emi Iustiniani Card. Seredi.)

Collectanea S. Congregationis de Propaganda Fide, 2 vols., Romae: Typographia Polyglotta S. C. de Propaganda Fide, 1907.

Corpus Iuris Canonici, ed. Lipsiensis secunda, post Aemilii Richteri curas . . . instruxit Aemilius Friedberg, 2 vols., Lipsiae, 1879-1881.

Corpus Iuris Civilis, 3 vols., Berolini: apud Weidmannos, 1928-1929; Vol. I, *Institutiones,* ed. stereotypa decima quinta, quas recognovit P. Krueger; *Digesta,* ed. stereotypa decima quinta, quae recognovit T. Mommsen et retractavit P. Krueger; Vol. II, *Codex Iustianus,* ed. stereotypa decima, quem recognovit et retractavit P. Krueger; Vol. III, *Novellae,* ed, stereotypa quinta, quas recognovit R. Schoell, et absolvit G. Kroll.

———, with the Glossa of Accursius, 5 vols., Lugduni: Hugo a Porta, 1553-1557.

Decretum Gratiani emendatum et notationibus illustratum cum glossis, Gregorii XIII, Pont. Max., iussu editum, 2 vols., Romae, 1582.

Decretales D. Gregorii Papae IX, suae integritate una cum glossis restitutae, cum privilegio Gregorii XIII, Pont. Max., et Aliorum Principum, Romae, 1582.

Gothofredus, Jacobus, *Codex Theodosianus cum perpetuis commentariis,* 6 vols., Lipsiae: M. G. Weidmann, 1736.

Haenel, Gustavus, *Lex Romana Visigothorum,* Berlin, 1849.

Hinschius, Paulus, *Decretales Pseudo-Isidorianae et Capitula Angilramni,* Lipsiae, 1863.

Jaffe, Phillipus, *Regesta Pontificum Romanorum ab condita Ecclesia ad annum post Christum natum MCXCVIII,* ed. 2, correctam et auctam auspiciis Gulielmi Wattenbach curaverunt S. Loewenfeld, F. Kaltenbrunner, P. Ewald, 2 vols., Lipsiae, 1885-1888.

Liber Sextus Decretalium D. Bonifacii Papae VIII, suae integritate cum Clementinis et Extravagantibus, earumque Glossis restitutis, Romae, 1582.

Mansi, Joannes, *Sacrorum Conciliorum Nova et Amplissima Collectio,* 53 vols. in 60. Parisiis, 1901-1927.

Schroeder, H. J., *Canons and Decrees of the Council of Trent,* St. Louis: B. Herder Book Co., 1941.

Reference Works

Beste, Udalricus, *Introductio in Codicem,* 3 ed., Collegville, Minn.; St. John's Abbey Press, 1946.

Bouscaren, T. Lincoln-Ellis, Adam, *Canon Law,* 2 revised ed., Milwaukee: The Bruce Publishing Co., 1951.

Buckland, W., *A Text of Roman Law,* 2 ed., Cambridge: at the University Press, 1932.

Bouix, D., *Tractatus de Judiciis Ecclesiasticis,* 2 vols. in 1, Parisiis, 1855.

Cicognani, Amleto, *Canon Law,* 2. ed., Reprint, Westminster, Md.: The Newman Press, 1949.

Coronata, Matthaeus Conte a, O.F.M. Cap., *Institutiones Iuris Canonici,* 2. ed., 5 vols., Taurini: Marietti, 1939-1947.

De Angelis, P., *Praelectiones Juris Canonici,* ad methodum Decretalium Gregorii IX exactae, 5 vols., Romae et Parisiis, 1877-1891.

De Luca, Joannes Card., *Theatrum Veritatis et Justitiae,* 15 vols. in 8, and Index Vol., Coloniae Agrippinae, 1706.

Doheny, W., *Canonical Procedure in Matrimonial Cases,* 2 vols., Vol. I, *Formal Judicial Procedure;* Vol. II, *Informal Procedure,* 2. ed., Milwaukee: The Bruce Publishing Co., 1948.

Goyeneche, S., *De Processibus,* 1 vol. in 2 parts, Romae: ad S. Ioannis Lat. .

Kearney, Raymond, *The Principles of Delegation,* The Catholic University of America Canon Law Studies, n. 55, Washington, D. C.: The Catholic University of America, 1929.

Krol, John, *The Defendant in Contentious Trials,* The Catholic University of America Canon Law Studies, n. 146, Washington, D. C.: The Catholic University of America Press, 1942.

Lega, Michaele Card., *Praelectiones de Iudiciis Ecclesiasticis,* 4 vols., Romae, 1896-1901.

Lega, M.-Bartoccetti, V., *Commentarius in Iudicia Ecclesiastica iuxta Codicem Iuris Canonici,* 3 vols. and Appendix volume, Romae: Anonima Libreria Cattolica Italiana, 1950.

Martin, Thomas Owen, *Adverse Possession, Prescription and Limitation of Actions: The Canonical "Prescriptio,"* The Catholic University of America Canon Law Studies, n. 202, Washington, D. C.: The Catholic University of America Press, 1944.

Migne, J. P., *Patrologiae Cursus Completus, Series Latina,* 221 vols., Parisiis, 1844-1855.

Noldin, H.-Schmitt, A., *Summa Theologiae Moralis,* 27 ed., 3 vols., Oeniponte/Lipsiae; Sumptis et Typis Feliciani Rauch, 1940-1941.

Noone, J., *Nullity in Judicial Acts,* The Catholic University of America Canon Law Studies, n. 297, Washington, D. C.: The Catholic University of America Press, 1950.

Noval, Joseph, *Commentarium Codicis Iuris Canonici,* Lib. IV *De Processibus,* 2 vols., Romae: Augustae Taurinorum, 1920-1932.

Ottaviani, Alaphridus Card., *Institutiones Iuris Publici Ecclesiastici,* 3 ed., 2 vols., Civitate Vaticana: Typis Polyglottis Vaticanis, 1947-1948.

Pirhing, Enricus, *Ius Canonicum in Quinque Libros Decretalium,* 5 vols. in 4, Dilingae, 1722.

Prümmer, O. P., *Manuale Iuris Canonici,* 6 ed., Friburgi-Brisgoviae, Herder Publishing Co., 1933.

Reiffenstuel, Anacletus, *Ius Canonicum Universum,* 5 vols. in 6, ed. novissima, Romae, 1831-1834.

Roberti, F., *De Processibus,* 2 vols., Romae: Apud Aedes Facultatis Iuridicae ad S. Appolinaris, 1926.

——, *Codicis Iuris Canonici Schemata, Lib. IV, De Processibus,* in Civitate Vaticana: Typis Polyglottis Vaticanis, 1940.

Salazar, F. - Fuente, V., *Procedimientos Eclesiasticos,* 4 vols., Madrid, 1868.

Santi, Franciscus, *Praelectiones Iuris Canonici,* 4. ed., 5 vols., Ratisbonae, 1886.

Schmalzgrueber, Franciscus, *Ius Ecclesiasticum Universum,* 5 vols. in 12, Romae, 1843-1845.

Sherman, C. - Robinson, T., *Roman Law Readings,* 2 vols., New York: Baker Voorhis & Co., 1933.

Van Hove, A., *Prolegomena ad Codicem Iuris Canonici,* 2 ed., Mechliniae, Romae: H. Dessain, 1945.

Verano, F. G., *Juris Canonici Universi Commentarius Paratitlaris,* 5 vols., Monachii, Sumptibus ac Typis Joannis Jaechlini, Typographi Electoralis et Bibliopolae, 1703-1708.

Wahrmund, Ludwig, *Quellen Zur Geschichte des romischkanonischen Processes Im Mittelalter,* 4 vols., Innsbruck: Verlag der Wagner'schen K. K. Universitats-Buchhandlung, 1905-1928; Vol. 5, Part I, Heidelberg, 1931.

Wenger, Leopold, *Institutes of the Roman Law of Civil Procedure,* Revised ed., New York: Veritas Press, 1940.

Wernz, F. - Vidal, P., *Ius Canonicum ad Codicis Normam Exactum,* 7 vols. in 8, Romae: Apud Aedes Universitatis Gregorianae, 1923-1938.

Woywod, S. - Smith, C., *A Practical Commentary on the Code of Canon Law,* Revised and enlarged ed., 2 vols., New York: Joseph Wagner, Inc., 1948.

ALPHABETICAL INDEX

Absence, 33

Administrator, 45

Advocate, 12

Allegations, 25

Apparitor, 49

Appearance in trial,
  spontaneous, 7, 8, 65, 66
  impossibility of, 12
  personal, 12

Benefice, 46

Bill of Complaint, 1, 17, 25, 38, 39, 76

Citation of witnesses, 61, 62

Command of Judge, 21, 76

Competence, 23, 25, 40, 69

Constable, 49

Contumacy, 12, 30, 31, 34, 56, 59

Defendant,
  incapacitated, 41
  identity of, 51
  individual, 40
  moral persons, 41, 45, 46
  subject to court, 17, 26, 35

Defendor of the bond, 11, 13

Delegation, 24, 71

Domicile,
  change of, 70

Edictal Citation, 49, 58
  use of, 59, 70

Effects of Summons, 64
  moment when realized, 69, 70, 72, 74, 75, 76

Formal Procedure, 10

Guardians, 41

Ignorance, 32

Incompetence, 40

Identity, 51

Invalidity, 29, 35, 57, 60, 63

Invitation to appear, 21

Judge, 23, 24, 36
  collegiate, 37, 38, 76
  individual, 37
  presiding, 30, 37, 38

Legitime peracts,
  of canon 1725, 66

Mails, the, 49, 50, 56

Messenger, 36, 49

Methods of,
  service of summons, 35, 48
  customary in U. S., 50, 56
  substitute, 49, 50, 76
  principal, 49

Newspapers, 47
  diocesan, 60
  public, 61

Nullity, 3, 5, 7, 13, 27, 29, 65

Parents,
  when cited, 41

Peremptory effect of summons, 30, 31, 32

Place of trial, 27, 28

Plaintiff, 26
  notice to, 48
  and contumacy, 48

Prescription, 64, 72

Presumption, 31, 33

Procurators, 12, 33, 46, 47, 50

Promotor Iustitiae, 11

Proof of Service, 51, 55

Publication of the process, 61

Religious, 44

Return Receipt, 57

Rogatory Commission, 52, 53

Roman Law, 31, 34

Sentence,
- execution of, 5, 6
- nullity of, 4, 5

Signatures, 30, 37, 39, 52

Summons,
- alternate recipients of, 54, 55
- definition of, 19, 20
- division of, 19
- effects of, 64
- knowledge of, 32, 33
- nature of, 20
- necessity of, 1, 5, 7, 11, 76
- not required, 7, 8, 9
- perceptive, 22
- proof of service, 51, 55, 57
- refusal to accept, 56
- service of, 35, 50, 76
- substantial element of trial, 17
- validity of, 24

Summary Procedure, 13
- judicial, 14
- necessity of summons, 17, 18, 76
- nullity, 15, 18, 76
- omission of solemnities, 15

Time of trial, 29

Trial,
- definition of, 17
- nullity of, 3, 4, 7
- substantial element, 17

Tutors, 41

Vocatio in ius, 1, 76

Weak-minded, 43

BIOGRAPHICAL NOTE

Victor M. Goertz was born on June 9, 1928, at Red Rock, Texas. He received his elementary education in the parochial school of Sacred Heart Parish, Rockne, Texas. His four years of high school and a year of college preparatory to studying for the priesthood were spent in St. John's Minor Seminary, San Antonio, Texas. In the Major Seminary Department of that same school he received his philosophical and theological training. On May 31, 1952, he was ordained to the priesthood in the Church of the Sacred Heart, Rockne, Texas. In September of the same year he was admitted to the School of Canon Law of the Catholic University of America, from which he received the degree of the Baccalaureate in Canon Law in June, 1953, and the degree of the Licentiate in Canon Law in June, 1954.

CANON LAW STUDIES*

358. Sesto, Rev. Gennaro J., S.D.B., A.B., S.T.L., J.C.L., Guardians of the mentally ill in ecclesiastical trials.
359. Carroll, Rev. James J., A.B., J.C.L., The bishop's quinquennial report.
360. Curtin, Rev. William Thomas, A.B., J.C.L., The Plaint of nullity against the sentence.
361. Ganter, Rev. Bernard J., J.C.L., Clerical attire.
362. Goertz, Rev. Victor M., J.C.L., The judicial summons.
363. Heintschel, Rev. Donald E., A.B., J.C.L., The medieval concept of an ecclesiastical office.
364. Kelliher, Rev. Jeremiah Francis, S.A., A.B., S.T.L., J.C.L., Loss of privileges.
365. Mock, Rev. Timothy, C.M.M., J.C.L., Disqualification of electors in ecclesiastical elections.
366. Smyer, Rev. Francis Anthony, A.B., J.C.L., Canonical regulations regarding exposition of the Blessed Sacrament according to canons 1274 and 1275.
367. Wiggins, Rev. Urban C., A.B., J.C.L., Property laws of the State of Ohio affecting the Church.

---

*For a complete list of the available numbers of this series apply to the Catholic University of America Press, 620 Michigan Ave., N. E., Washington (17), D. C., for a general catalogue.

www.ingramcontent.com/pod-product-compliance
Lightning Source LLC
LaVergne TN
LVHW050157080826
844660LV00012B/309

* 9 7 8 0 8 1 3 2 2 5 2 9 6 *